ENGLISH ❖ HERITAGE

Book of
Prehistoric Settlements

ENGLISH ✠ HERITAGE

Book of
Prehistoric
Settlements

Robert Bewley

B.T. Batsford Ltd/English Heritage
London

'To Jill, Hannah, Fiona and Richard'

First published 1994

Typeset by Lasertext Ltd, Stretford,
Manchester M32 0JT
Printed and bound in Great Britain by
The Bath Press

Published by B. T. Batsford Ltd
4 Fitzhardinge Street, London W1H 0AH

A CIP catalogue record for this book is
available from the British Library

ISBN 0 7134 6857 2 (cased)
0 7134 6853 x (limp)

Contents

List of Illustrations   7

List of Colour Plates   9

Acknowledgements   10

Preface   11

1 Introduction   13

2 Discovery and dating   19

3 The Early Years   32

4 Early Farmers and Neolithic Settlement   45

5 Bronze Age settlement   65

6 Iron Age settlement   91

7 Conclusions   132

Sites to Visit   135

Further Reading   139

Index   141

Illustrations

1 Knook Camp, Salisbury Plain, Wiltshire 14
2 Division between the Highland and Lowland zones of Britain 16
3 Map extract showing Antiquities 20
4 Swarthy Hill, Cumbria 21
5 Section through an ancient ditch 22
6 Sites silt up and are ultimately revealed as crop marks 23
7 Maiden Castle Iron Age hillfort, Dorset 24
8 Geophysical survey 26
9 The radiocarbon calibration curve 27
10 A dendrochronological sequence 28
11 A pollen diagram, from Barfield Tarn, Cumbria 29
12 Barfield Tarn from the air 29
13 Reconstruction of the land bridge with the European mainland after 7000 BC 30
14 Distribution of Mesolithic sites in Britain 34
15 Model of Mesolithic settlement 36
16 Excavations at Oronsay 36
17 Location map of Star Carr and the Mesolithic sites in the North York Moors 38
18 Model for clearance of woodland 41
19 Broomhill, one of the few structures from the Mesolithic period 42
20 Bowman's Farm settlement, Hampshire 43

21 The spread of farming into Europe 44
22 The Sweet Track, a Neolithic wooden trackway 46
23 Reconstruction of the Meare Heath Bow 46
24 Wooden artefacts from Ehenside Tarn, Cumbria 47
25 Plasketlands, Cumbria, a Neolithic site 48
26 Windmill Hill, Wiltshire, a Neolithic causewayed camp 50
27 Four possible groups of Neolithic interrupted ditch systems 51
28 The distribution of causewayed camps in England 52
29 Hambledon Hill from the air 53
30 Plan of the causewayed camp at Etton 56
31 Skara Brae, Orkney 57
32 Plan of the Neolithic settlement at Barnhouse, Orkney 58
33 Neolithic house at Balleygalley, Northern Ireland 60
34 Crop marks of a Neolithic house at Balbridie, Scotland 61
35 The excavations at Balbridie from the air 62
36 Belle Tout, Beaker settlement 66
37 Extract from the Bodmin Moor survey plan 68
38 Aerial photograph of Bodmin Moor 69
39 Leskernick, Bodmin Moor, Cornwall 70

40 Dartmoor: part of the Dartmeet parallel reave system on Holne Moor 72

41 Dartmoor: Ripon Tor on Horridge Common, showing the parallel reaves 73

42 Rider's Ring, a Bronze Age settlement on Dartmoor 74

43 Shaugh Moor Enclosure 15, Dartmoor 75

44 Trethellan Farm, Cornwall 77

45 Reconstruction of the Bronze Age settlement on Itford Hill, Sussex 78

46–8 Black Patch, Sussex 79–80

49 Location of settlements and deposits of weaponry at the confluence of the Thames and Kennet rivers 81

50 Aerial photograph of the crop marks at Mucking, Essex 81

51 Paddock Hill, Thwing, North Yorkshire 82

52 The excavation plan of Paddock Hill, Thwing, a Bronze Age settlement 83

53 Lea Green, Grassington, North Yorkshire 84

54 Standrop Rigg, Linhope, Northumberland 85

55 Woden Law, Roxburghshire, a palisaded settlement and cord rigg 86

56 Alyth Burn, Perthshire. Aerial photograph of circular houses 87

57 Plan of the prehistoric houses at Alyth Burn, Perthshire 88

58 Stonehenge area 88

59 Winterbourne Stoke, near Stonehenge, plans of houses 89

60 The Stonehenge landscape from the air 89

61 The location and names of Iron Age tribes 92

62 Plan of the Iron Age enclosures at Woodbury and Little Woodbury 93

63 Little Woodbury as photographed by OGS Crawford 94

64 The excavation of the round house at Pimperne, Dorset 95

65 Maiden Castle, Dorset 96

66 The distribution of Iron Age hillforts in England 97

67 The distribution of Iron Age hillforts in Wales 98

68 Hod Hill, Dorset 99

69 Hillforts in Wessex with theoretical territories based on Thiessen polygons 100

70 The landscape of the Fens from the air 102

71 Belsar's Hill, ringwork in the lowlands of Cambridgeshire 103

72 Hod Hill, Dorset 104

73 Tre'r Ceiri hillfort on the Lleyn peninsula, Wales 105

74 Yeavering Bell, Northumberland 106

75 Plan of the hillfort at Ingleborough, North Yorkshire 108

76 Orientation of entrances of Iron Age houses 109

77 Reconstruction of life in a round house at Carn Euny, Cornwall 110

78 An early aerial photograph of Ladle Hill, Hampshire 111

79 Ladle Hill showing the associated linear features 112

80 Danebury, Hampshire, from the air 113

81 Danebury area: an extract from a survey of aerial photographs 114

82 Quarley Hill, near Danebury, Hampshire 115

83 Pimperne, Dorset 116

84 Aerial photograph of Pimperne 18, Dorset 117

85 'Antenna enclosure' at Brechfa, Llandissilio, Wales 118

86 Collfryn, Wales, a defended enclosure from the air 118

87 Collfryn, Wales, excavation plan 119

88 Staple Howe, North Yorkshire 120

89 The internal structure of Dun Telve broch 121

90 Reconstruction of a crannog 122
91 Glastonbury Lake Village 123
92 Sutton Common, South Yorkshire 125
93 'I expect you have heard about Roman roads' 126
94 Location of sites and excavations by the Oxford Archaeological Unit in the Thames Valley 127

95 Excavation plan of the Iron Age enclosures at Watkins Farm and Mingies Ditches 128
96 Area near Stanton Harcourt in the Thames Valley 129
97 Aerial photograph of part of Skomer Island 130

Colour Plates

Between pages 64 and 65

1 Buckland, Oxfordshire
2 Crop marks of a late Iron Age and Romano-British site at Wolsty, Cumbria
3 Reconstruction of a Mesolithic settlement
4 Pike O'Stickle, Langdale, Cumbria
5 Bodmin Moor, Cornwall. Rough Tor stone-built hillfort
6 Stowe's Pound, Cornwall
7 Aerial photograph of the reconstruction of the Bronze Age settlement at Flag Fen, Cambridgeshire
8 Reconstruction of an Iron Age hillfort

9 Aerial photograph of a low-lying Iron Age hillfort at Wardy Hill, Cambridgeshire
10 A 'banjo' type enclosure, at Ashton Keynes, Wiltshire
11 Butser Hill Ancient Farm, Hampshire
12 Reconstruction of the Iron Age settlement, Thorpe Thewles
13 Airport Catering site, Stansted, a reconstruction
14 Glastonbury Lake Village from the air in 1966
15 Reconstruction of part of the settlement at Chysauster, Cornwall
16 Broch of Gurness, Orkney

Acknowledgements

Without the initial request to write this book from Stephen Johnson and the enduring support of my wife, Jill, this book would not have been possible. The help of archaeologists in Britain and Ireland has been a great bonus, many have willingly offered information, advice and illustrations. I am grateful to David Buckley, Tim Champion, Mark Corney, Peter Crew, Andrew Fleming, Frank Green, JD Hill, Terry James, George Lambrick, David Miles, Diana Murray, Chris Musson, Adrian Olivier, Rog Palmer, Mike Parker Pearson, Francis Pryor, Peter Reynolds, Colin Richards, Blaise Vyner and Humphrey Welfare for their help, discussions and comments. Particular thanks are due to John and Bryony Coles for all their help and encouragement and the information about Glastonbury Lake Village. I am also very grateful to Stephen Johnson and Peter Kemmis Betty for their comments on earlier drafts of the text.

The following institutions and individuals provided photographs and illustrations: Mr R. Besley, Bill Britnell of Clwyd-Powys Archaeological Trust, Cambridge University Collection of Air Photographs, Cleveland Archaeology Section, John and Bryony Coles, Chris Cox, Peter and Lysbeth Drewett, Derek Edwards, Essex County Archaeology Section, Andrew Fleming, Frank Green, Jim Hancock, Dennis Harding, Terry James, Terry Manby, Chris Musson, the Ordnance Survey, Oxford Archaeology Unit, Derek Simpson, Ian Ralston, Peter Reynolds, Ben Robinson, Royal Commission on the Historical Monuments of England, Royal Commission on the Ancient and Historical Monuments of Scotland, and Geoff Wainwright. A special debt of gratitude is owed to the RCHME (especially Clare King) and RCAHMS for assisting with the provision of so many aerial photographs and plans. The work of Judith Dobie in English Heritage and David Williams on the illustrations deserves special praise and thanks.

Preface

A book which covers such a broad topic as prehistoric settlements cannot cover all the subject and has to be selective. This book is no exception. It is not intended to be a catalogue of settlements in Britain; that would be a task worth doing but not the purpose here. The picture presented is in some ways a reflection of my own discovery of archaeology which has centred on survey and settlements, but it is also a reflection of current thinking about archaeology and the constant need to interpret and re-interpret the past. Archaeology is not a static subject and new information, through survey and excavation, means that we have constantly to update our thinking and approaches. Sometimes these new discoveries are accidental and immediately force us to change our perceptions; at other times the revelations derive from archaeological projects which have taken a decade or more to provide us with a new approach.

The book also concentrates on England, which is more a reflection of my knowledge and not in any way meant to reduce the importance of Scotland, Wales and Ireland, whose prehistoric archaeology is amongst the best in western Europe. Further reading for these countries is listed at the end. The Palaeolithic period has been left out completely, not through any lack of interest but because it requires a complete book to itself.

Many archaeologists are moving away from the Three-Age system of stone, bronze and iron, because these technological changes are not equivalent to all the changes in the archaeological record. They are, however, convenient divisions for dividing up the settlement evidence so long as they are not seen as watersheds in prehistory. The gradual changes which took place throughout the prehistoric period are evident from the settlements, burials, ritual and industrial sites.

1

Introduction

the past must be Invented
the future Must be
revIsed
doing boTh
mAkes
whaT
the present Is
discOvery
Never stops

A mesostic by John Cage

As a guide to prehistoric settlements this intro-
ductory chapter shows the way in which
archaeology has thrown light on 'prehistory'
and how we have arrived at the present definition of 'settlements'. There is a plentiful supply
of traditional guides to prehistoric archaeological sites and these are listed under further
reading.

The purpose of this book is to answer four
basic questions:

1　Where are the prehistoric settlements of
　　Britain?
2　What form do these settlements take?
3　How old are these sites and landscapes?
4　How do archaeologists study settlements?

The first three questions are the most frequently asked of any prehistorian and therefore
it is justifiable to present this book as an answer
to some of these questions. The fourth question
will be answered as a theme running through
the book. Examples of the way in which
archaeologists use their data and manipulate
it (not without contention) appear in every

chapter. Some of these will be familiar; for
example, radiocarbon dating is now a widely
understood technique. Other techniques such
as dendrochronology or spatial analysis using
Thiessen polygons may be less familiar.

There are no absolute answers in archaeology
and especially in prehistory. Archaeology as a
discipline can provide a framework on which
to hang various interpretations. The study of
prehistory is a comparatively new subject; the
term prehistory was first used as a title to a
book, *Pre-historic Times* by John Lubbock (later
Lord Avebury) in 1865. The hyphen between
the 'pre-' and 'history' is important as the term
conflicted with religious (western) beliefs in
challenging the antiquity of the Earth and
Man's place within it. Lubbock was asking
questions which we today are still trying to
answer; some of the more straightforward ones
about date are being answered, but the questions of social structure and political organisation are subject to the same prejudices and
fashions which Lubbock had to fight against in
1865. The intellectual atmosphere when he was
writing was very different from today; Darwin's
Origin of Species was still four years away from
being published (1869). Lubbock was bringing
concepts about the antiquity of Man to a
readership thoroughly imbued with the date of
creation as 4004 BC. 'The first appearance of
man in Europe dates back to a period so remote,
that neither history, nor even tradition, can
throw light on his origin, or mode of life.'
Others at the time (Palgrave in this case),

13

1 *Knook Camp, Salisbury Plain, Wiltshire. Salisbury Plain has areas of chalk grassland in England which have not been ploughed for over 2000 years, and the survival of earthworks is therefore very good* (Cambridge University Collection of Air Photographs: copyright reserved).

whom Lubbock quotes say, 'We must give it up, that speechless past; whether fact or chronology, doctrine or mythology; whether in Europe, Asia, Africa or America; at Thebes or Palenque, a Lycian shore or Salisbury Plain; lost is lost; gone is gone for ever' (**1**).

This book is about that 'speechless past' and how for the last 130 years people have not given up studying it but have been trying to find out more about it. Although beyond the scope of this book, it is interesting to contemplate why as a species, *homo sapiens sapiens*, we are so interested in our past; we seem to have an innate desire, even a need to know from whence we came.

Prehistory took over 50 years to become accepted in the wider popular terminology; a local society was formed in 1908 called the Prehistoric Society for East Anglia and in 1935 this became the national Prehistoric Society. This Society is now an international organisation with over 2000 individual members from professors to practising archaeologists, but the bulk of the membership is the interested amateur (see further reading for more information

about the Society and its publications). Despite the obvious interest in prehistory the revised education system in England, introduced in 1991, does not allow the teaching of prehistoric archaeology as a core subject. The arrival of the Romans is the starting point for teaching British history; it is hoped that readers of this book will be able to use it to redress this classical imbalance.

Archaeology and prehistory have their own imbalances; it can be argued that the majority of prehistory, at least until the Iron Age, is based on the study of the dead. This is mainly due to the very good survival of the monuments which were erected for the dead: long barrows, round barrows, dolmens, chambered tombs and passage graves. The study of settlements is a much more recent research topic but no less interesting for that. However, the distinction between the living and the dead, settlement and ritual is a modern construction. We have to be aware that what we might interpret as a particular category of site might have performed several functions which involved both the everyday 'domestic' functions as well as the 'ritual' functions or vice versa. The sites known as 'causewayed enclosures' are included here not because we know that they were settlements or were ritual sites but because they are important (non-burial) sites within the society of the time – and so are part of the landscape which included settlements. They have been included because we do *not*, in all honesty, know what they are (**26, colour plate 1**). Defining their use might be as difficult as defining the use of a parish hall if there were not the records to show the many uses of a hall, most of which have nothing to do with ritual (Christian) activities in the strict sense of that term.

Another imbalance concerns the material which prehistorians have at their disposal. There are no written records to give an insight into the ideas and activities of these communities; there are only the material remains of past societies, that have not completely decayed, and it is only a proportion of these material remains which are recovered by the archaeologist. This is a fundamental point to stress: the prehistorian does not know what the total recoverable amount of material there is or was. Therefore, the sample we have to deal with is a sample of a sample, the total size of which can never be known. Added to this are the raw data, the bones, stones, organic material (leather, wood, and environmental information), which survive in different locations at different rates; in the technical jargon the 'post-depositional factors' coupled with 'site formation processes' (the study of how the material left at a site was deposited) are very important to the prehistorian. With every interpretation, be it functionally, environmentally or socially determined, the first question is whether the pattern which has been revealed is as a result of deliberate human activity or as a result of more than 2000 years of decay and disruption.

This can apply as much to individual sites as it can to landscapes, and it would have been possible to change the title of the book to include the word 'landscape'; prehistoric people had their own cognitive geography of their landscape. Ours is different and we have imposed our own semi-scientific ideas on landscapes in an attempt to understand their formation, geologically and archaeologically. If we take the evidence from the Somerset Levels or the Fens of East Anglia to gain some understanding of prehistoric life, we are able to show what life in prehistoric times was like in those areas, but it does not give us the total picture for Britain. We cannot extrapolate from the low-lying peat of the Levels to the highlands of Dartmoor or Bodmin, or the chalklands of southern and eastern England, or further afield to Scotland or France, even though the settlements may be contemporary.

Fox's *Personality of Britain*, published in 1932, influenced a generation of archaeologists and affected the way they conceived the British Isles. He proposed a distinction between a Highland Zone and a Lowland Zone as a good starting point for understanding early settlement (**2**). Apart from extensive use of distribution maps, which are fundamental to so many archaeological studies, his Zones were meant to reflect cultural differences. His approach is seen now as too environmentally deterministic, despite its influence on many archaeologists. In 1972 Chris Taylor, echoing Fox, proposed a Zone of Destruction and a Zone of Survival for Britain. He was taking a somewhat provocative stance in saying that the recovery of the pattern of settlement of pre-Saxon societies in Britain is something that archaeologists cannot achieve. The geographical techniques which archaeologists borrowed from geography to study settlement patterns did not work for prehistoric Britain because we cannot ever know what the total pattern was; therefore we do not know if what we have recovered is 1 per cent or 99 per cent of what was originally there. Except in the Fens in East Anglia, which have been shown to contain the near-complete Romano-British pattern, Taylor argues that the prehistoric pattern is never obtainable. Survey work since 1970 has considerably enhanced our understanding of the prehistoric settlement of the British Isles in both the Zone of Destruction (through aerial photography and excavation) and the Zone of Survival (through terrestrial and aerial survey).

This recent survey work has gone a long way to redress the balance of information; more often than not the archaeological distribution map of settlements tells us two things:

1 Archaeologists have surveyed an area, i.e. the picture we have is not a true one of where people lived but a reflection of where surveys have taken place.

2 The validity of the results is further reduced because they are also a reflection of the extent of destruction (or masking) since prehistory. A good example is the belief that the majority of settlement in Wessex was on the tops of the downland; the valley bottoms being devoid of archaeological remains. This

15

Caithness

Shetlands

Orkneys

Caithness

Outer Hebrides

Highlands
of
Scotland

Belfast
Lough

Southern Uplands

Cheviot Hills

Lake
District

Pennine Chain

I. of Man

N. York.
Moors

Yorkshire
Wolds

R. Trent

Lincoln
Wolds

Anglesey

Lleyn

The Fens

Wicklow
Mountains

Cambrian Mountains

Cotswold Hills

Chiltern Hills

R. Thames

North Downs

Mendips

Salisbury
Plain

South Downs

Exmoor

Bodmin
Moor

Dartmoor

I. of Wight

Scilly Isles

Division between high and low land

2 *The division between the Highland and Lowland zones of Britain* (after Fox, *Personality of Britain*).

has been shown to be incorrect and much of the early activity has been masked by soil movement off the tops and into the valley bottoms, sometimes with over 2m (6ft) of soil.

From this discussion it is clear that every site exists within a landscape, but how do we define landscape? As a tract of countryside on which is inscribed the palimpsest of marks left by different generations of human activity? The emphasis is on the landscape as the countryside and *not* the marks which are left on it. This is a fundamental part of understanding prehistoric settlements, that the landscape setting has changed in the course of prehistoric time; it is also important to attempt to understand how and when these changes to the landscape occurred.

Recent research work by the author in the northern part of Cumbria started off finding out where the sites were; this was done using a combination of documentary research and aerial photographs. The difficulty lay in attempting to understand their location in a landscape context, and this involved finding out what date they were and understanding the changes to the landscape in that time span. To understand prehistory it is important to appreciate the time depth. The span of this book is over 8000 years, or 200 generations (if a generation is taken at 40 years); anyone who has studied history, especially family history, will appreciate what 200 generations represents.

Why are archaeologists obsessed by time and chronologies? In prehistory we want to know the age of a settlement to the nearest 200 years (or perhaps 100 years by the late Iron Age). Three of the sites excavated in Cumbria ranged in date from 3400 bc (**8, 25**) through to 500 bc (**4**) and ad 100 (± 150–200 years). Occupation in this instance has been going on for over 5500 years and probably continuously, although settlements in the Bronze Age are hard to find in this part of Cumbria. For the interested layman or student of a local area the location of sites was in part determined by the fluctuat-ing sea-levels which we know had risen and fallen in the past 5500 years.

Archaeologists used to try to define 'prehistoric cultures' as if they would conform to a network of peoples across the British Isles. This has now gone out of fashion because so many new scientific and theoretical avenues of research have opened up. With the increase in excavations and study of material from excavations (especially environmental information which tells us about the climate, flora and fauna in the past), it is becoming increasingly clear that broad generalisations about prehistoric settlement throughout the whole of Britain do not stand up to scrutiny when examined at the local and regional level. Similarly the large-scale climatic changes are only a part of the much more important local shifts in weather. These local changes, both human and natural, are becoming the focus of much archaeological research; the question which needs to be answered is why certain groups of people adopt certain behavioural characteristics and others do not, and how far these groups can be called cultures.

Richard Bradley warns that 'prehistorians pay too high a price when they screen out so much local variation'. Is this local variation a 'cultural difference'? If so, how do we define prehistoric cultures? Prehistorians infer a relationship between the material objects and human behaviour. 'Prehistory is an anonymous study: reconstruction of prehistoric cultures depends on a knowledge of the relationship that exists between material objects and human behaviour in living cultures' (Glyn Daniel, *Idea of Prehistory*). This 'knowledge of the relationship' has been called into question and forms an important part of current research. It does, however, make prehistory a subjective study and one which has to cope with the study of change through time and the diachronic perspective makes it an exciting challenge.

The use of 'theoretical models' is one way in which order can be obtained; the models are not static nor are they the truth. Any model is an attempt at reconstruction and therefore if some of the building blocks are changed, a new radiocarbon date for example, the model will have to be rebuilt. This process of continuous re-assessment is at times frustrating, but it also ensures that the subject never stands still; re-interpretation of settlements is a theme which will run throughout the book.

The title of this book is similar to Richard Bradley's *The Prehistoric Settlement of Britain* and it might be argued that he has said it all anyway. Fortunately the intervening 15 years has seen a large amount of new material; the basics are of course the same, but the work which has taken place at sites which he mentions as 'work in progress' has now been published and new sites are being discovered and worked on (for example Somerset Levels and Flag Fen). New techniques in their infancy in 1978 are now standard practice (for example, dendrochronology). There has been a shift away from trying to define prehistoric cultures and a move towards finding and trying to understand prehistoric land-use and landscapes.

It is not always the best way to conduct research to extract one aspect of life (settlement) from the whole gamut of human existence; however it can be justified if an attempt is made to promote the study of that element because it has been neglected for so many years. An alternative title might have been 'prehistoric landscapes' because the interconnection between all aspects of prehistoric life could have been examined more closely, but by focusing on the settlement aspect of prehistoric landscapes it has been possible to show the diversity of settlement types and locations.

Death has been the main focus of so much

prehistory, and it can capture the public's imagination (remember Lindow Man, the bog body from Cheshire?); discovering and understanding settlements does not have the same immediate appeal but the question 'where did they live?' is one of the most frequent questions archaeologists are asked.

All those connected with archaeology feel a responsibility towards the sites and landscapes which they encounter; either to preserve them for posterity or, if this is not practicable, to record as much as possible about the site prior to destruction. Similarly land-owners, farmers and everyone who visits sites also have a responsibility, akin to a steward, to maintain sites so that they do not become damaged or littered with unwanted material. The sites and landscapes mentioned in this book are often in private ownership. A good way to see most of these is from the air, which only requires permission from air traffic! Visiting the sites on the ground requires permission from the landowner and this is the best way fully to appreciate sites.

I have tried to find a balance between representing sites and landscapes which can be visited or at least 'experienced' and those which are part of the archaeological literature, which cannot be visited as they have been destroyed or are on private land or only show as crop marks. Too often knowledge is trapped in too few places; often these are public places but the vast majority of the public are not aware that these archaeological sites exist. There is a changing attitude amongst professional archaeologists (myself included) and this book is offered in the hope that it may bring more information about sites to a wider audience.

2
Discovery and Dating

The first question posed in the introduction was 'Where are the prehistoric settlements?'. Imagine a map of Britain with no archaeological information on it; how do archaeologists obtain the information to fill the map up? The purpose of this chapter is to show how the map can be filled up with information relating to prehistoric settlements, from single find-spots to whole landscapes. As mentioned in the last chapter, this is not the true settlement pattern of prehistoric settlements but the current state of knowledge.

To provide an adequate answer to this question we have to look where sites are, how archaeologists have discovered them, and why there are blank areas. More often than not, the distribution of archaeological sites is as much a reflection of survey techniques and recovery strategies as it is a reflection of past human land-use and settlement. There are, however, a number of notable exceptions and the more comprehensive the archaeological surveys of Britain become, the greater our understanding of prehistoric (and later) settlement and society will be.

The work of antiquarians is an important element in the development of the current picture of prehistoric sites and settlement. The very visible, and in some ways understandable, sites, especially Bronze Age round barrows, were the focus of antiquarian attention; the campaigns of Mortimer and Greenwell in the nineteenth century, to name but two barrow diggers, meant that barrows and not the settlement evidence were seen as representative of prehistoric society.

Camden's *Britannia*, published initially in 1587 and later in a number of editions, is the first attempt to describe the antiquities of Britain. This approach, to list all sites and monuments, is still very much with us today; records are kept within each county and for each country in National Records (see below).

In the 1695 edition of Camden's *Britannia* (a translation from Latin) there is scant mention of what happened before the Romans arrived and the little attention it receives is shrouded in biblical and classical references. If we look at Dartmoor, an area now known as one of the richest archaeological areas in the country, Camden says only that there was a forest there. Gibson, who translated *Britannia* adds that 'The river Dert first runneth thro' Dertmore, a large forest 20 miles long and 14 broad. It was first made a Forest by K. John and had anciently in it many tinn-works. It now yields pasture every summer to near 100,000 sheep.'

This illustrates two crucial points: the first is that the landscape is ever-changing in terms of its appearance, even over a few centuries. Secondly archaeological interpretations change with each generation; we would like to imagine our latest ideas, theories and data are the best yet, but only time can prove us right or wrong and new information will change the way we perceive the past.

It was not until William Stukeley (1687–1765) that prehistory received some attention; the main theme of his work was the pre-Roman period. Stuart Piggot, an authority on Stukeley, writes: 'After his death in 1765 we have to wait until the nineteenth century before we can find men taking up the tradition of archaeological fieldwork where he left it, and until the twentieth century before the worth of his work was realised.'

3 *Map extract showing Antiquities (Map 81 Cheviot) Reproduced from the 1980 Ordnance Survey 1:50,000 Landranger map* (permission of the Controller of Her Majesty's Stationery Office, Crown Copyright).

The antiquarian beginnings, although providing a nucleus of information on which we can build, also provided archaeology with some of its techniques of analysis – pottery typologies, relative chronological sequences and an approach to comprehensive cover of the whole country. Admittedly they were dealing with a much smaller sample, there were few excavations and no crop-mark sites, but the idea of making a record for the whole country was prevalent in the late sixteenth and early seventeenth centuries.

The work of the antiquarians during the seventeenth, eighteenth and nineteenth centuries, in terms of excavations and surveys,

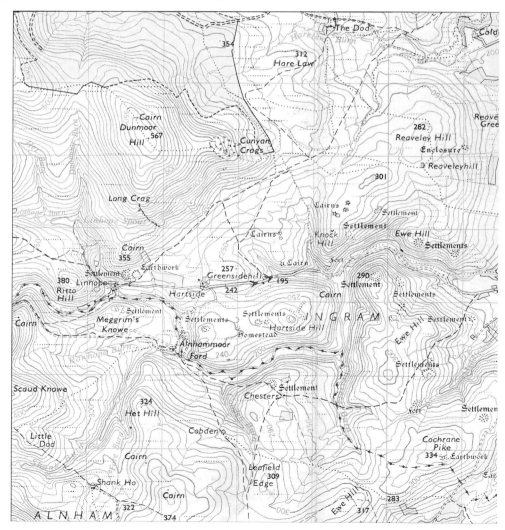

began to bear fruit in the twentieth century with the establishment of archaeology as a subject in its own right. Universities started to teach it and in 1908 survey bodies for England, Scotland and Wales were established with the grand titles of Royal Commissions for the Ancient and Historical Monuments. (The addresses are listed at the back of the book.) The relevance here is that they provide a national database from which to extract information at a national level. For example in Scotland, in the Royal Commission's National Archaeological Record, there are 2202 records for prehistoric settlements with perhaps a further 1000 records which could be included in any corpus on prehistoric settlements. The purpose of presenting these figures is to show that we have information about thousands of sites, often no more than a location and perhaps an aerial photograph. What we are lacking, for the most part, is a comprehensive understanding of the date and function of these sites.

This is obviously a crude search mechanism at a national level but it is a beginning for any particular study. At a more detailed level every county in England has a Sites and Monuments Record (SMR) from which information on a particular site can be obtained. Wales and Scotland have similar arrangements which are more regionally based, whereas in Northern Ireland the records are held centrally. The Republic of Ireland, through its Office of Public Works, has recently finished a County by County Register of all sites. These records, at national and local level are the up-to-date equivalents of Camden's *Britannia* and are invaluable resources for any student of archaeology.

The information contained within these records is the result of years of accumulated information from all possible sources; the major primary source was the Ordnance Survey Archaeology Division records, set up by one of the pioneers of archaeological field survey, O.G.S. Crawford, in the 1920s. Ordnance Survey maps are an invaluable resource (**3**) for prehistoric settlement archaeology. Although

some well-preserved sites are depicted, the value of the maps lies in the topographical information about a site or an area.

One example is the Solway Plain, Cumbria, where the known crop-mark and earthwork sites which were thought to be Roman or later left the author wondering where the prehistoric settlements sites could have been. Analysis of the 1st Edition Ordnance survey maps showed that about 30 areas of former peat bogs had been drained in the nineteenth and twentieth centuries, and it could be argued that these areas of bogs were an important resource for prehistoric people. Fieldwork and excavation proved this to be the case as well as dating some of the crop marks to the prehistoric period (**4, colour plate 2**).

Survey techniques

Although excavation has played an important part in revealing prehistoric settlements it is only after surveys have been carried out that

4 *Swarthy Hill, Cumbria. A triple-ditch Iron Age hillfort overlooking the Solway Firth on a sand-cliff* (Crown Copyright).

excavation can take place. Archaeological survey has a range of techniques and approaches and is fundamental in any landscape study.

Documentary research

Archaeological survey begins at a desk, searching the literature and maps for any reference to archaeological sites in an area; this may involve making requests to the National Archaeological Record, the local Sites and Monuments Record, the Public Record Office, and libraries to chase up references. For the historical periods documentary research takes on a new meaning as original documents have to be examined, read and understood. In all archaeological survey work it is important to find out the nature of any previous work.

Aerial photographs

All areas of Britain have aerial photographs which are of immense value in discovering and locating archaeological sites. These photographs are of two types – vertical or oblique.

5 *Section through an ancient ditch showing the taller growth of the crop above the ditch* (photograph copyright of Aerial Archaeology Publications: Derek Edwards).

Vertical photographs are rarely taken for specifically archaeological purposes, but by chance they contain a wealth of archaeological information. A recent survey by Royal Commission on the Historical Monuments of England (RCHME) of an area of 2500km^2 in the Yorkshire Dales examined 11,000 vertical photographs from which over 10,000 archaeological records were created.

The largest collection of vertical photography was produced from 1945 to 1948 when the RAF carried out a National Air Survey (partly to keep the pilots occupied after the Second World War). Millions of photographs were taken and stored in London; these are now available for consultation through the relevant national aerial photographic collections and libraries agencies (addresses at the back).

Oblique photographs are held in national and local collections and these have been taken by archaeologists as part of aerial surveys all over Britain. A major source (of obliques and verticals) is the Cambridge University Committee for Aerial Photography (CUCAP) where a collection of archaeological photographs has been created since 1945 by one of the pioneers of aerial photography, Professor J.K. St. Joseph.

Readers interested in examining their local area can contact these organisations with requests to look at the available photography.

The purpose of archaeological aerial survey is to locate sites which only show from the air and to record sites and buildings which can be recorded to their best advantage from the air. Many textbooks describe the techniques of aerial photography (see Further Reading), but the phenomenon of crop marks should be explained as so many prehistoric settlements are revealed in this way (**5, 6**). Where a ditch has been dug and subsequently filled up, the ditch fill will hold more water and nutrients than the surrounding soil. The crop above the ditch will grow taller and ripen later than the crop surrounding it; when this is viewed from the air it usually shows as a darker mark in the

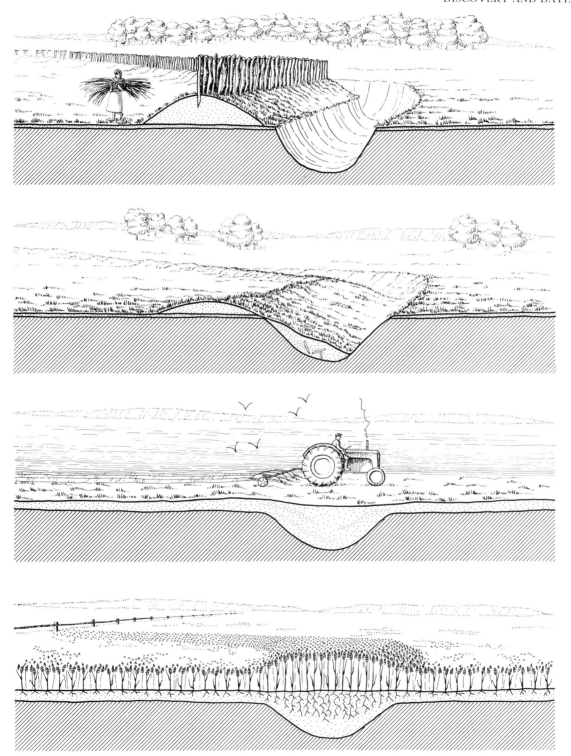

6 *Representation of the way in which sites silt up, become levelled and are ultimately revealed as crop marks* (copyright: West Yorkshire Archaeology Service; drawn by Angela Grove).

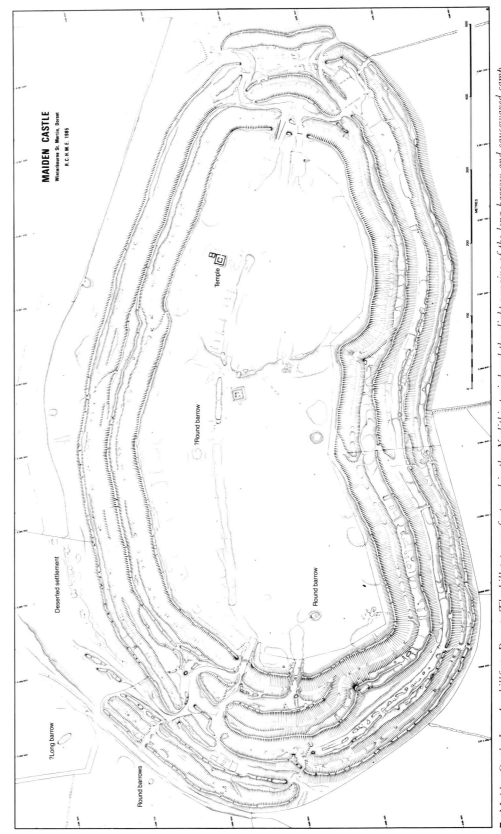

MAIDEN CASTLE
Winterbourne St. Martin, Dorset
R.C.H.M.E. 1985

Temple

?Round barrow

Round barrow

Deserted settlement

?Long barrow

Round barrows

METRES

0 100 200 300 400 500

7 *Maiden Castle Iron Age hillfort, Dorset. The hill top was first used in the Neolithic period and the slight remains of the long barrow and causewayed camp are just visible. In contrast the massive ramparts are some of the most impressive in England* (Crown Copyright RCHME).

field and the size and shape of sites can be recorded (**5; colour plates 1 & 2**).

Serendipity, luck and the weather play an enormous part in archaeological research, and this is especially true for aerial photography. The dry summers of 1949, 1959, 1975, 1976, 1984, 1989 and 1990 allowed for the discoveries of thousands of new sites. But this is not a new phenomenon; in *Pre-historic Times* Lubbock wrote about the year 1853: 'In consequence of the extraordinary dryness and coldness of the weather during the winter months of 1853, the rivers of Switzerland did not receive their usual supplies, and the water table in the lakes fell much below its ordinary level, so that, in some places, a broad strand was left uncovered along the margin.' In this margin 'specimens of human workmanship' were discovered; this was the beginning of the study of 'Lake Dwellings', prehistoric villages situated on the edge of lakes. This Swiss work was to inspire Munro to survey the Scottish lochs and tarns and led to the discovery of a new settlement site type, the 'crannog' (see below).

Field survey
The weather has as much to do with archaeological discoveries as good organisation and research designs. Less dependent on chance, but still subject to the vagaries of the weather, are the techniques which involve what has become known as 'field survey', examining sites on the ground, through fieldwalking (walking ploughed fields to collect artefacts) or using surveying equipment (theodolites and more modern instruments which electronically measure distances) to make detailed plans of known archaeological sites (**7**).

Another aspect of field survey, is the use of geophysical measuring equipment (magnetometers and resistivity machines) – often referred to as remote sensing. These machines measure differences of magnetism or electrical resistance in the soil; where the soil has been disturbed the magnetism and the electrical resistance has changed and these changes can be detected (**8**).

It is also possible to measure the differences in the geochemistry of the soil; for example an area high in phosphates might be one where intense domestic occupation has taken place or where cattle have been quartered. Measuring for these traces is highly labour intensive but can yield some interesting results.

Excavation
Finally small-scale excavation plays an important part in discovering and understanding prehistoric sites. Often the most detailed field survey, using all the techniques above can record the site but it cannot give a date or any insight into its function. Small-scale excavation can provide a date for a site be it from a radiocarbon date or from artefacts discovered during the excavations. To quote from a recent newsletter of the Prehistoric Society (PAST), Professor Barry Cunliffe reported on the Danebury Environs Project (this is after 20 seasons at the Danebury hillfort): 'What is clear is that a comparatively small intervention in the field, so long as it is guided by a carefully framed research design and pre-informed by high quality air-photographs and magnetometer surveys, can be extremely productive of new information. At this rate . . . our preconceptions of 1st millennium society are likely to change quite significantly.'

Dating
There are two ways in which archaeological material can be dated. The first is by relative means, that is by association with artefacts dated in a typological series. The second is by absolute dating, using scientific techniques such as radiocarbon dating and dendrochronology.

Relative dating methods
Before the absolute dating methods had been discovered the only means of dating a site, be it a small enclosure or a large city, was by relative dating. On an excavation the sequence of occupation can be determined by the stratigraphic relationship between the various layers

Plasketlands, Cumbria

Magnetometer data

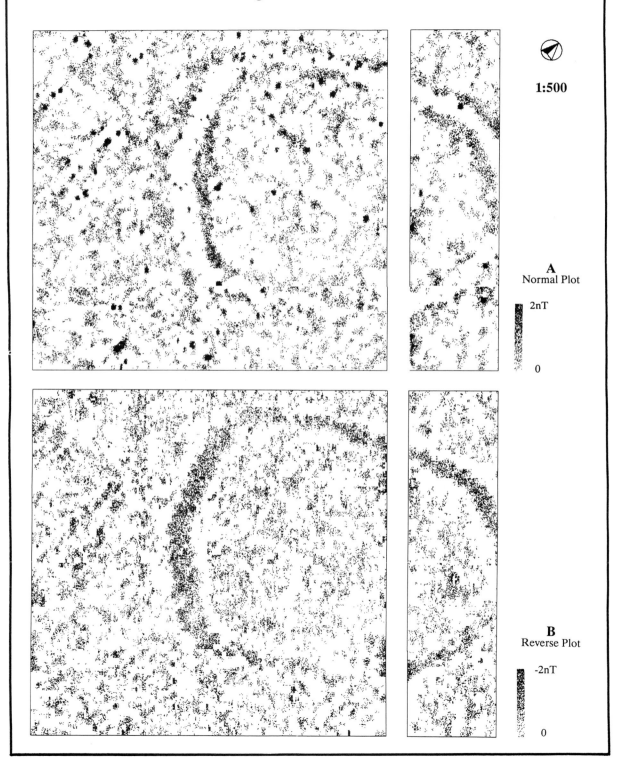

1:500

A
Normal Plot

2nT

0

B
Reverse Plot

-2nT

0

and features. Similarly the artefacts which are excavated can be placed in a typological series, often showing the development of a pottery style, or metalwork style. Typology can give a sequence of events but rarely, unless the artefacts can be linked with historical dates, can it give an absolute date. The sequence is relative to other sequences and its true beginning and end could often only be guessed at unless it can be tied to a known historical event from written sources. In prehistoric Britain this is hardly ever the case as writing was not part of life until the late Iron Age.

Absolute dating methods

Perhaps the greatest advance in archaeology this century was the discovery of the **radiocarbon dating** technique in 1958. As with all new discoveries there was a period of euphoria and expectation that this new technique would answer all the dating problems in archaeology. Scientists were aware that there was something not quite right with radiocarbon dating, especially when dating artefacts of a known historical date. It was not until dendrochronology, as a technique, had been developed that the full impact of radiocarbon could be realised.

Radiocarbon dating is possible because the radioctive carbon atoms in all organic material decay at a known rate; this 'half-life', used to calculate a radiocarbon result, is the Libby half-life of 5568 years (Libby was the discoverer of radiocarbon dating). Radiocarbon years are given in uncalibrated years BP, where 0 BP is defined as AD 1950. The error term, $\pm$, should be quoted to 1 sigma (68% chance of being correct). Results and error terms are rounded to the nearest 10 radiocarbon years for error terms of greater than $\pm$ 50 years, and to the nearest five if smaller. Recently a new way of measuring the amount of radioactive carbon, called accelerator mass spectrometry (AMS) has been

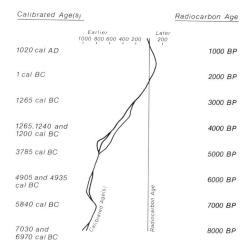

9 *The radiocarbon calibration curve.*

developed; by this method the number, or a proportion of the number of C14 atoms is measured in the sample relative to the C13 and C12 atoms. This adds to the accuracy of the technique.

The major assumption of radiocarbon dating was that the background radiation throughout prehistoric (and historic) time was constant. This assumption was not found to be incorrect until artefacts of a known historical were radiocarbon dated and the discovery of a complementary and equally important technique, dendrochronology.

Dendrochronology is the dating of wooden artefacts and trees through the patterning of the tree-rings. This enables samples of wood of a known date (via dendrochronology, see below) to be radiocarbon dated; a calibration curve was created against which 'radiocarbon years' could be calibrated against real years (**9**). The final limitation to radiocarbon dating was the age of artefacts it could date; given the half life decay of carbon there had to be a limit on the very old things that radiocarbon could date; this limit is approximately 50,000 years.

Dendrochronology was developed for climatological studies and is based on the knowledge that trees produce an annual growth ring but that the distance between each ring is not constant; the growth each year depends on the climate (sunshine, rainfall and temperature).

8 *Geophysical survey showing the plan of a Neolithic site, possibly a settlement, at Plasketlands in Cumbria.*

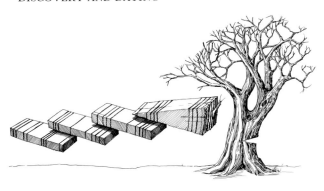

10 *A dendrochronological sequence.*

Therefore, the pattern of rings for a tree's life will be similar to other trees in the same area or of the same date (**10**). A databank now exists from the present day going back 8000 years matching up the various patterns and sequences of tree rings. The discovery of long-lived trees in the Californian desert (bristle-cone pine, *Pinus aristata*) enabled the sequence of patterns to be stretched back to about 8000 years (about 7000 for oaks, *Quercus* sp.).

Without radiocarbon, dendrochronology would be an enormous advance in itself but could only be used where wood had been preserved. Coupled with radiocarbon dating, however, it enabled the calibration of the absolute tree-ring date to the radiocarbon date to be made. This inevitably showed that the amount of radiocarbon in the atmosphere was not constant and that at certain times there was considerable change in radioactive levels. Two high-precision laboratories (Belfast and Seattle), using different conventional radiocarbon techniques and different tree species, have independently produced curves which agree across a number of 20-year timespans. Belfast has produced a calibration curve going back to 5210 BC. The calibration of radiocarbon dates is a science in itself, but simply put the advent of dendrochronology has made the radiocarbon dates too young. Any calibration curve may have a wiggle which is pronounced enough to allow two possible dates for any single charcoal sample. Thus for any one sample it is possible to have at least two dates. This often means that radiocarbon dates are quoted as 2337–2360 or 2232–2349, as possible dates.

All the work in radiocarbon dating is based on probability theory; there is either a 68% chance (one standard deviation) to determine the age or there is a larger time band at the 95% level, or two standard deviations. Radiocarbon dates are published in many different ways; as calibrated dates (BC, for calendar years Before Christ) or if they have not been calibrated using the b.c., or b.p. convention, which denotes radiocarbon years before Christ or before present. All radiocarbon dates are published with 'standard deviations'. The deviation is the range in which the date is likely to fall and the confidence level is the statistical confidence we can have in the date falling within that range.

The archaeological journal *Antiquity* uses the agreed 1986 standard and the lower case b.p. for uncalibrated dates and small BP for calibrated dates. Some authors use the convention RCY (radiocarbon years) after a date; others use 'cal BP' for calibrated and small capitals BP for uncal. In 1993 a new calibration curve was introduced and the editor of *Antiquity* suggested new conventions; c14 for radiocarbon, TL for thermoluminescent date and UT for uranium/ thorium dates. The presentation of radiocarbon dates is confusing; my only advice is to handle all dates with care looking for a BC, bc or BP, bp and if the dates are uncalibrated or calibrated. In this book I have had to use the dates which have been published; so some are calibrated and some not.

Environmental studies

One of the important advances in the natural sciences in the last 50 years has been the way in which soil and sediments can be analysed; the aim of the analysis is to find what is contained within the archaeological deposits which is not immediately visible to the naked eye. By studying the microscopic and macroscopic remains in sediments the details of the

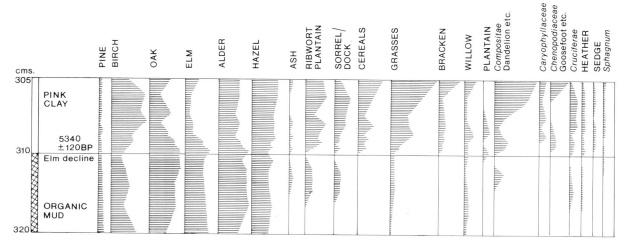

11 *Pollen diagram, from Barfield Tarn, Cumbria.*

site formation processes, mentioned in the introduction, can be better understood. Techniques of flotation (washing soil in water and skimming of the material which floats) have been developed so that small fragments of bone, seeds and macrofossils can be identified. Similarly sampling strategies have been developed for pollen analysis.

The study of pollen grains (palynology) was developed by a Swede, Lennart van Post, in 1916, initially for forest trees but as the techniques developed it helped to identify all pollen-liberating vegetation. Large numbers of pollen grains are suspended in the atmosphere

12 *Barfield Tarn from the air; tarns and bogs provide good sediments for studying past climatic changes* (copyright: the author).

and will be preserved when deposited in anaerobic conditions (peat deposits especially). If soil samples of archaeological or palaeoenvironmental deposits are taken and examined through a microscope the identification of the pollen grains can indicate the different types of vegetation (especially trees) which had been growing at or near that particular place. The samples are taken throughout the stratigraphic sequence of a site or peat bog and thus a 'history' of the vegetation at that site can be presented from the pollen evidence (**11, 12**).

One episode on a European scale which pollen analysis has identified is the 'elm decline' at about 3000 bc; there have been many debates about what caused this widespread decline in elm. Was it as a result of prehistoric clearances for settlements and fields? Or was it the dreaded elm-beetle which carried a disease which killed the elms? Or was it a climatic change which affected elms? The answer has to be a combination of all three but it is unlikely that elms were selected for clearing when there was a rich variety of trees; the arguments for selective use of elm leaves for fodder will also be looked at later.

Larger macrofossils are also isolated from the archaeological deposits so that studies of seeds and insects can be made. These analyses inform us about the types of crop grown (if any), the insects which lived there and the microfauna (small animals) which fed off the debris left by prehistoric peoples. The insects can be good indicators of climate; a good example is the work in the Somerset Levels where the studies of beetles informs us about the climate of the day and complement the pollen and plant macro-studies. Dung beetles are good indicators of large herbivore activity.

If we return to the blank map of what is now the British Isles and take it back to 12,000 bc, the present east coast does not exist and the British Isles are part of the European continent (**13**). By about 6000 bc the sea-level rose to cut-off the land bridge and form the North Sea. The rise in sea-level was due in part to melting

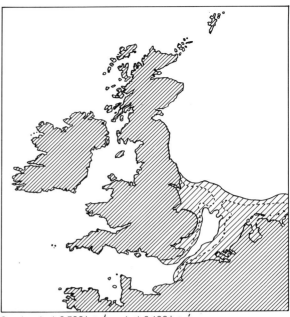

Sea level at 6,700 b.c. / and at 6,400 b.c. /

13 *Reconstruction of the land bridge with the European mainland after 7000 BC. The British Isles have been rising in the north-west and sinking in the south-east since the end of the last glaciation.*

ice but also to the dipping of the land; the west and north of the British Isles was (and still is) rising whilst the south and east are sinking. This has implications for the discovery of sites before the land bridge was closed; many Mesolithic sites are under the North Sea. The occupants of many of these sites will have travelled to the North York Moors and all along the current east coast of England. Thus the sites which we do find in these areas are only a small part of the total picture. It is unlikely we will ever be able completely to excavate one of the sea-bed sites, though more are being discovered and recorded (see **14**).

There are a number of ways in which we can conceive the past; one is through supposed cultural groupings – cultures like the Halstatt or La Tène; or we can use the technological classifications of stone (Palaeolithic, Mesolithic and Neolithic), bronze (Bronze Age) or iron (Iron Age). Or we can use the environmental

Table 1 Vegetational Zones of the Late and Post Glacial.

bc	Name	Zone	Vegetation
12,000			
	Older Dryas	I	Park tundra
10,000			
	Allerød interstadial	II	Birch with Park tundra
8800			
	Younger Dryas	III	Park tundra
8300			
	Pre-Boreal	IV	Birch, Pine forest
7600			
	Early Boreal	V	Hazel, Birch, Pine
7000	Later Boreal	VI	Hazel, Pine
			a) Elm, Hazel
			b) Oak, Elm
			c) Oak, Elm, Lime
5500			
	Atlantic	VIIa	Mixed Oak Forest Alder, Oak, Elm, Lime
3000			
	Sub-Boreal	VIIb	Alder, Oak, Lime. Elm decline
500			
	Sub-Atlantic	VIIc	Alder, Oak, Birch

distinctions as in Table 1. These are based on vegetational and climatic changes which took place and have names or Roman numerals to distinguish them.

The technological terms – Mesolithic, Neolithic, Bronze Age, Iron Age – are used here as a loose framework on which to hang 8000 years of prehistory. It is widely recognised that they are as meaningless as referring to the late twentieth century as the 'computer age' or the 'car age' but as they have gained such wide acceptance they are useful labels. The changes in technology did not denote dramatic and instant cultural changes; through the long periods of prehistory cultural changes took place, and these are reflected to some degree in prehistoric settlements. Defining what we mean by 'prehistoric cultures' is an interesting subject and the difficulty of studying human behaviour is the extent to which our 'material culture' (pottery, personal objects, houses, etc.) reflects the 'tribe' or group to which we belong.

3

The Early Years

What do we mean by settlements? Is it a term for the individual settlement (including the houses and ancillary buildings) or is it the areas or landscapes in which prehistoric people settled and lived? I have interpreted it as a combination of both; that is the landscapes in which people have lived and also, where necessary, a detailed analysis is presented of those few settlements which we know about. This has opened the way to mentioning sites and types of sites which may not be settlements in the strict sense, as often prehistoric settlement areas are defined not by the discoveries of houses but by the distribution of non-settlement information (burial cairns for example). Especially for early prehistory it is necessary to take a broad view.

As we saw in the previous chapter, since the nineteenth century archaeology has been helped (and hindered) by Montelius' Three Age System – Stone Age, Bronze Age and Iron Age. This system has been a useful framework for conceptualising the past as progress from stone technologies to the metalwork of later periods. It is embedded in the belief that technology is the motivating force of progress and that time inevitably means progress. The fact that we use word-processors and drive around in sophisticated pieces of machinery does not mean we have 'progressed' as a civilisation; it simply means we think we have greater control over our lives than was the case in prehistory.

In the early post-glacial years, survival in a new and changing environment was the challenge which faced the colonisers from the south and east. The picture which I would like to portray is how people lived. The starting point will be the arrival of new settlers once the final ice (at least until the next Ice Age) had retreated and finish with the arrival of the Romans. The introduction of different technologies does not *in itself* affect the settlement pattern distribution and therefore the changes which took place in prehistory throughout Britain, in terms of settlement, will be dealt with chronologically. This has its problems in that the Mesolithic in southern England can be seen to end in the fifth millennium BC but in parts of northern England and Scotland carried on into the third millennium BC or later. Generalisations are difficult to sustain and each area or region should be examined in greater depth than I have been able to delve.

It is worth stressing that life in earlier prehistoric times was very different from today; it was not, as the nineteenth-century writers would have us believe, a time of wild barbarians and savages. The people, *Homo sapiens sapiens*, were the same as we are today. The difference was that their everyday life was almost completely involved in their own survival. Finding, killing, gathering, and obtaining food and shelter were the daily priorities; in fact it is no different today except that we receive money to do a particular job or task and pay someone else to kill the animals, collect the vegetables, build and heat the house. The use of fire was a long-established skill and must have played an important part in the daily life. The popularity of camping today is perhaps in part due to the 'back-to-nature' desire many people have; if you examine the spacing of tents and caravans in a field it gives an insight into the way people will 'occupy' an area.

The backdrop for prehistoric settlements is the landscape of Britain after the retreat of the glaciers (15,000–12,000 BC) and after the country had been re-settled. The return of *homo sapiens sapiens* was accompanied by herds of elk, reindeer, horse and red deer with the demise of larger mammals such as mammoth, bison, woolly rhinoceros, elk and lion. The retreat of the ice and the colonisation of new faunal and floral species happened over a period of a few thousand years; not least because of the fluctuations in the re-advances and retreats of the ice between 15,000 and 10,000 BC. The important point is that, once the various animal and plant species had established themselves, there began a period of occupation in the British Isles which has remained uninterrupted since. The only major change during the last 12,000 years has been the separation of the British Isles from the continent in about 6000 BC (**13**); a break which has now been joined by the Channel Tunnel. *Vive l'Europe!*

The first phase of settlement has left little trace and is a continuation of a Palaeolithic (Old Stone Age) way of life based on hunting and gathering. The main focus for settlement may have been caves but there were also 'open' sites; these sites are much harder to find than caves and we have a distorted picture of Palaeolithic life in Europe. Caves and a number of occupation sequences from this period have been discovered; not surprisingly the caves of south-west England, Wales, and the Mendips were occupied first. However the north was also colonised, at Victoria Cave in north Yorkshire and Kirkhead Cave in southern Cumbria.

There can be no doubt that other sites from the early recolonisation period will be found, not least the 'open' sites in low-lying areas. Many of these will be under the North Sea and the Channel and are therefore well protected from the archaeologists' intentions to excavate them (if not protected from dredging and fishing activities), but further research on this type of site would shed light on these early settlers.

The Mesolithic

By about 8000 BC the population had expanded sufficiently that open sites in a variety of locations were being established. Other changes had taken place as the climate ameliorated, notably the growth of woodland; the pine and birch woodland which provided suitable habitats for the wild ox, red deer, roe deer and wild pig were exploited. Similarly the retreat of the ice left a landscape which is hard to imagine today, but one which contained many areas of open water. The Lake District is a good example in England, as are the lochs and loughs of Scotland, Wales and Ireland: all the water in these lakes and upland tarns is a remnant of the last glaciation.

Sometimes the smaller lowland tarns survive today (**12**) but generally they have become overgrown with peat and are either bogs, or have been drained and are now part of the agricultural landscape. These areas of open water were numerous and not always large but they were the local resource centre – the supermarket of the Stone Age. Around them the animals and birds would congregate for water and food and fish (which still happens today) and as the human race is essentially lazy (or will take the most effective course of action in the short term) the easiest place to hunt and fish would be around these tarns and lakes (except when at the coast). Fish, as a resource for these hunter-gatherers (fishing is a combination of both hunting and gathering), has been much underrated and the survival of many of the early prehistoric communities depended on freshwater and marine resources.

14 *Distribution of Mesolithic sites in Britain* (sources: various).

At one site, Culver Well, in Portland, Dorset, a large shell midden with lean-to shelters, has had over 7250kg (16,000lb) of shell excavated. It has been estimated that this is the equivalent of 2,550,000 calories; given that a family of eight requires about 17,400 per day there would have been enough calories for 150 days. The excavated part of the midden only represents one fortieth of the site. Thus our concepts about mobile hunter-gatherer populations has to be revised when sites such as these are excavated. John Wymer, a leading authority on the Mesolithic period, quotes some similarly interesting statistics on the enormous waste of a shell-fish diet; it has been estimated that one red-deer carcase is the equivalent in food values to 52,267 oysters. Apparently 700 oysters would have to be eaten every day, in the absence of any other food, yet only 1400 cockles or 400 limpets would provide our daily nutritional needs. The further away one gets from written history the more one has to rely on abstract statistics and extrapolations to attempt to understand prehistoric society. Fish, in contrast to shell fish, is highly nutritious, and easily obtainable. The many coastal Mesolithic communities will have caught and eaten salmon, sea trout and whole variety of fish, the remains of which are unlikely to have survived, given their fragile nature.

Hunter-gatherers is the name for people who did not farm, grow crops or keep animals. They collected food by hunting, and gathering wild fruits, nuts and any edible plants. The name also indicates the type of settlement which they may have used. That so few hunter-gatherer (Mesolithic) sites have been found should be no surprise (**14**). From the end of the Palaeolithic period and well into the Neolithic period this way of life was the predominant mode. It leaves little trace except for the stone tools and only exceptionally evidence of settlement and houses. The Mesolithic period is the story of middens or flint scatter sites.

Not surprisingly, the coast played an important part in the settlement pattern of hunters and gatherers from 8000 to 4000 BC. The sea-level was much lower than today, 52–36m (170–120ft) lower from 7000 to 5000 BC (**13**); at 5000 BC the sea-level stabilised at a similar level to the present day. Many early Mesolithic sites are now submerged in the east of the country but can be found on the 25ft (8m) contour in the west.

There are a number of dated sites from the coast in the Atlantic period when the climate was on average 2°C warmer; although this is not a great fluctuation in climate it is enough to make a significant difference for habitation in upland areas. From the distribution map (**14**) the dispersed settlement pattern can be seen but this is not a true reflection of the settlement pattern; too many factors do not allow us to recover a representative pattern as yet.

Territorial analysis

It is possible to model the pattern at a local level with the use of 'site catchment analysis'. Site catchments are defined as a specific area around a site; the area can be defined in terms of time or distance from a base camp (for example) to a hunting site; usually for early prehistoric sites the definitions are 1km (0.6 mile) and 5km (3 mile) zones, or the length of time estimated it would take to travel these distances. A modern analogy would be the siting of supermarkets on the edge of towns; their location is determined by a number of factors but the proximity of a large population within easy reach of the shops is fundamental for the shopper and supermarket itself.

Hunter-gatherer activities can be seen as dispersed within a widening zone of concentric circles within a catchment zone centred around a focal point. The 'activity dispersal zones' would have overlapped as no activities are totally mutually exclusive, and indeed the sites need not be. The use of sites at different seasons for different purposes (hunting, base camp, killing, flint knapping etc) was obviously important, and models have been proposed for these early hunter-gatherer societies (**15**).

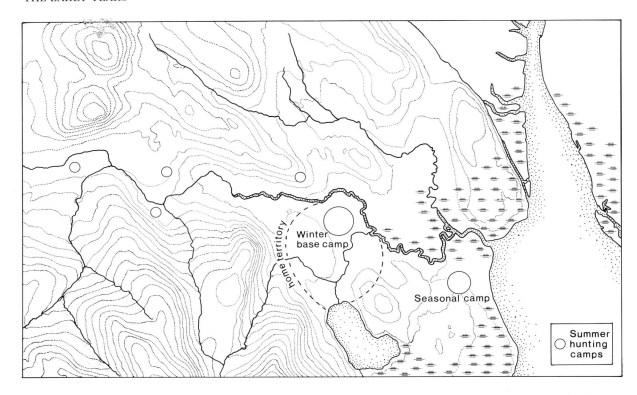

15 *Model of Mesolithic settlement* (after S. Palmer, T. Darvill and A. Whittle).

One of the most well-known and recently excavated sites is that of Oronsay (**16**). Oronsay is a small island of 14 sq. km (5.8 sq. miles) in the Inner Hebrides – 30km (19 miles) west of Scottish mainland at 56° North. The site consists of six shell middens – three of which had been identified in the nineteenth century and excavated between 1879 and 1913; the other three were identified in a programme of work undertaken by Paul Mellars from 1970. In all, it is a unique site in the British Isles. Five midden sites around the coast of Oronsay were excavated – looking for answers to a number of questions: was the island occupied continuously by a small resident population or was it an intermittent pattern of occupation by a variety of more mobile, wide ranging groups who were based on neighbouring islands or the mainland? Could such a small unit have survived as a breeding unit? What determined the choice of

specific locations? Why were the 'sites' re-occupied and re-used so specifically? Can we view five midden sites as 'occupation sites' in the usually accepted sense, or are they more like extraction areas where shellfish are processed at this central point? There is some evidence for hearths and hut structures at one midden site, Cnoc Coig. The shell middens were used over

16 *Excavations at Oronsay* (courtesy of Paul Mellars).

a relatively long time span, 700–800 years from *c.* 5000 to 4200 BC and then came to an abrupt end.

It is interesting that in the Mesolithic the archaeological evidence consists of middens and flint scatters. Shell middens are often the most informative type of site as they are the 'rubbish' from settlements which informs us about what people ate and what they threw away. Many settlements, as found by archaeologists, are just pale reflections of what actually took place on the sites. To understand human behaviour we have to study 'rubbish'.

Rubbish and middens

There is a project in the United States (and now Britain) which started life as the Tuscon Garbage Project. The American archaeologist who started this, William Rathje, now studies the modern 'land-fill' sites to inform local authorities on what is being thrown away and the effects of land fill deposition on certain objects. Coupled with this research was a series of interviews with the local population to find out what they thought they 'consumed' and what they actually threw away. This work has helped our understanding of any anthropological study – what people actually do and what they say they do are two very different matters. For example, if a man was asked how much beer he had consumed the amount was exaggerated; if a women was asked about her male partner's beer consumption, the figure would be less than what was actually found in terms of cans of beer in the rubbish bin. Similarly in a recent meat shortage in one area of America the amount of meat which was discarded (past its sell-by date) increased rather than decreased; people were hoarding meat and thus exacerbating the meat shortage!

Shell middens are therefore important as Mesolithic settlement evidence because they are the rubbish from a settlement. So what were they eating? Fish and shell fish in varying proportions were an important part of the diet; the percentage varied at Oronsay between the middens but mainly shellfish was eaten with the consumption of fish up to 65% in one phase of one midden.

At another well-known Scottish site at Morton in Fife near the mouth of the river Tay, occupied from 4300–5300 BC, the occupants had a much more varied diet; they hunted red and roe deer, aurochs and pig and also ate whelks and mussels. Seabirds were also caught (and probably eaten) as were some deep-sea fish, like cod and sturgeon, which would have needed a boat. The occupation at this site was spread over a large area and there is evidence for living structures, hearths and flintworking.

Most archaeological descriptions of the Mesolithic concentrate on the different stone-tools technologies and not the people nor the landscape they occupied. The inland sites do not often contain the organic remains which the coastal sites do and we have to rely on the stone technologies.

What the stone tools tell us is that in the eighth millennium BC people lived by hunting, with bows and arrows, a wide range of forest animals, such as red and roe deer, pig, elk and aurochs. There is also evidence that they trapped beaver, pine marten, wild cat and badger.

One area which has attracted much work on the Mesolithic sites has been the North York Moors and this is a good illustration not only of what there is to be found out about the early colonisation of post-glacial Britain but also of the biases which our methods of working impose on our understanding of the period.

We have already seen general models for the way they located their sites and Jacobi's model, below, emphasises the mobility and seasonality of sites. The area we today call the North York Moors is interesting in the Mesolithic period; its proximity to the east coast means that it was probably exploited to a greater degree for longer in the Mesolithic than any other upland area. If we remember the land-bridge with Europe (**13**), the population in the catchment area would have been large and it exploited the upland area for hunting. In northern England a number of types have been identified:

(a) seasonal sites, summer or winter hunting
(b) winter sites in lowland – Vale of Pickering, the Fylde, the Isle of Axholme and also along the Trent itself
(c) summer sites in North York Moors or Pennines.

Each community is estimated to have been perhaps 25 people or more.

Star Carr

This model can be supported by the original interpretation of the most famous of all British Mesolithic sites, Star Carr (**17**). Star Carr is situated in the low-lying Vale of Pickering only 8km (5 miles) south-west of Scarborough; the Vale is bordered north and south by higher ground; the North York Moors to the north and the chalk Wolds to the south.

The stone tool evidence suggests that 60 per cent of the retouched pieces at Star Carr are end scrapers and burins (that is, they were used for the processing of skins) whereas the higher sites in the North York Moors contained different assemblages, more archery type artefacts.

17 *Location map of Star Carr and the Mesolithic sites in the North York Moors. a = Maglemosian microliths; b = Maglemosian axe; c = Maglemosian bone point; d = Sauveterrian microliths, two reconstructed in wooden haf*

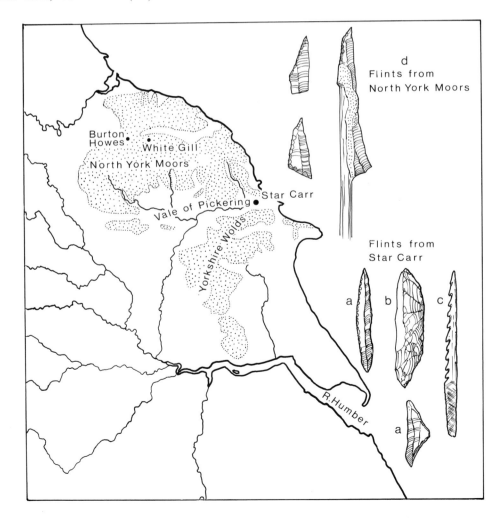

As mentioned earlier faunal remains are used to confirm or deny the interpretations from other sources. In the excavations at Star Carr, the excavator, Grahame Clark, was interested in (among other things) the time of year when the site had been occupied. He felt that the faunal assemblage (the bones of the animals left behind) would give him this information. The bone report concluded that the site had been occupied from October to April, i.e. autumn to spring; the evidence for this was the red deer skulls discovered at the site with antlers attached. As red deer shed their antlers in April the assumption was that the deer were hunted in the winter. As a result of this interpretation the site was seen as a winter base camp. The site was occupied in the eighth millennium BC; one radiocarbon date for the site is 7538 BC.

The site of Star Carr is one of the fixed points of British archaeology – every student has to know about it and as a consequence it has been re-interpreted at least nine times. The re-interpretations started with the excavator himself; again with the subject of seasonality as a major concern he was able to reinforce his model of migration of deer and humans from the winter base at Star Carr to the summer ranges of the North York Moors, the chalk Wolds to the south and even west to the Pennines. The other re-interpretations, from 1978 to 1988 suggested that the site of Star Carr was important not for red deer as meat resource but as raw material (antler) and that it was a kill site used all year round, or an industrial working site, the availability of water being important for soaking skins; or that the red deer migration theory did not work and the site was occupied in the early summer or all summer, or that the lack of fish, especially pike, was a not a winter indicator as Clark suggested but was a result of the rivers not yet being colonised; finally another interpretation has the site as a base camp because of the wide range of mammalian species and artefacts.

This confusing list is presented here to highlight the widely differing interpretations that can be assigned to one very important and well-excavated site. The number of re-interpretations inspired Legge and Rowley-Conwy to 'revisit' the faunal assemblage of Star Carr and their latest, and perhaps not final, interpretation is at least based on a complete re-assessment of the bones. Legge and Rowley-Conwy conclude that:

(a) the site was used only in late spring and summer;
(b) the red and roe deer animals were culled when they were either one or three years old;
(c) there was less meat available than originally estimated and therefore a reduction in the scale of occupation is necessary;
(d) the site was possibly a hunting camp, with the meat being removed to a base camp elsewhere.

In the space of 35 years the site of Star Carr, the most famous of all Mesolithic sites, has gone from being a winter base camp to a summer hunting site – all on the same evidence. This example is not meant to criticise in any way the scholars involved in the debate on Star Carr, it is meant to serve as an example of how archaeology operates. There is no final answer, as there might be in mathematics, because the evidence is open to interpretation. Star Carr was the forerunner of many future excavations in terms of the technique of excavation and presentation of the environmental and faunal data. New questions about faunal assemblages have risen since 1954 and it was inevitable the early excavation results would be reassessed. A recurrent theme throughout this book is the way in which reinterpretations of sites add to their interest and are part of how we come to know what we do about prehistory.

One of the questions which archaeologists ask of a bone assemblage is 'Which bones survive?'. Is it only the long bones for meat or are the bones a representative sample of the whole carcase? (It has to be remembered that the thinner, more fragile bones do not survive to the same extent as the thicker bones like the femur and astragalus.) Having answered these questions it is possible to obtain the minimum number of individual animals (MNI) at any site. In doing these analyses the faunal experts can make an assessment of whether a site was a 'kill' site or a consumer site and also at what time of year the site was in use. By analysing the fracturing of the bones it is possible to say whether the bones were gnawed by other animals (dogs in particular) or were consumed by humans.

Pattern of settlement

Where does this leave our understanding of eighth–sixth millennium archaeology? We still know that the predominant form of obtaining food was from hunting, fishing and gathering and that the whole of the British Isles (before it was separated from Europe in about 6000 BC) was occupied by a mobile population who made use of all types of resources from the sea to the uplands and also the lowlands. The problem is one of discovery; so many of the sites are probably under the North Sea or buried beneath subsequent peat growth. The discovery of sites from this period has depended largely on former antiquarian interest and now local amateur interest, and on the local weathering of the sites from buried peat. The good survival of flint means that one aspect of Mesolithic is over-represented in the archaeological record, and the evidence of settlement, the organic material is rarely found. The brushwood platform at Star Carr is one of the very few organic finds from this period.

The pattern of settlement is more a reflection of recovery techniques than it is a pattern of human settlement. The upland sites are generally situated on the tops of ridges and valley heads, overlooking natural basins where the movement of deer can be watched. There is evidence that forest trees above 350m (1150ft) were burnt down to keep the view clear. A drawing (rock art) from Cueva de los Caballos (Spain) shows 12 hunters with eight beaters driving a herd of deer towards the archers. This can be interpreted as a summer hunt as there are females and fawns and only one stag; the stag normally arrive in October for the rut.

There can be no doubt that rivers were important for the communities who depended on natural resources. The problem we have is finding the sites which were near rivers 8000 years ago. The water-drainage patterns were different from today, especially as the major rivers were still developing. At the micro-scale we need to look at the river bank and stream edges which were the edges then; in a few cases (for example in Teesdale) there are Mesolithic deposits eroding out of the existing river bank, but these instances are rare. The ever-changing course of the rivers means that tracing the original course is the first task and looking for the sites the secondary task. If we add to this the mobility of these people, lowland communities might have had 'territories' or catchment areas of up to 80km (50 miles), the difficulty of establishing the Mesolithic settlement pattern can be appreciated.

Estimating the total population of the British Isles in the Mesolithic is clearly difficult but it has been put at about 20,000 people, which is on the conservative side. There are few burials to help with identifying what the people looked like and what differences there might have been between communities in burying their dead.

If we conceive of the first phase of post-glacial colonisation as that from the retreat of the glaciers to the removal of the land bridge with Europe (6000 BC), it helps to place the context of the changes which happened after 6000 BC. During this first phase the sea-level had been rising as the ice was melting. This rise in sea-level meant that communities would be exploring new areas for colonisation as their normal hunting and fishing grounds were being removed by the sea. Therefore they began to expand further north in England and into Scotland. From 6000 BC onwards, because Britain became an island, the developments in

Dense forest of pine, birch, hazel and oak.

Grazing by animals, some forest clearance.

Hunters' camps, burning of trees.

Shrubs and trees cleared, more animals, less regeneration.

Land clear, soil degradation.

Partial reforestation.

18 *Model for clearance of woodland* (after Simmons).

technology are not affected by contacts across the land bridge with Europe. The flint technology changed to a smaller, geometric microlithic assemblage, possibly as part of a change in the types of missiles which were used. The woodland environment changed, too, with a more closed woodland, with oak, alder, lime and elm taking over from pine and birch.

It is logical to assume that the population density increased as the area available for settlement was reduced and therefore more communities further north are found after the land bridge had been closed. Similarly a wider range of resources was used which in itself would have brought about changes in technology.

Forest clearance by the mid-fifth millennium was beginning to affect soil and soil degradation; felling an oak, which can use several gallons of water a day, taking it up through the roots and losing it via its leaf system (transpiration), will affect the ground water. Waterlogging can occur in cleared areas and

the growth of peat has been shown to begin about 5500 BC at Kinder Scout in the southern pennines. Woodland clearance was a process which went on for over 8000 years and its effects have to be emphasised (**18**). Once trees have been felled the soil and water properties change and soil erosion is much more likely to occur. Environmental studies have shown the effect of human intervention in the uplands especially; when this is coupled with the climatic changes it is easy to see why the uplands are not the same as they were even 3000 years ago.

So far I have dealt with settlements as concepts, as part of the settlement system rather than as the places themselves. As has already been mentioned, the sites are often near water, be it a stream, river or the coast. The majority of sites in the Mesolithic are on sandy soils and many of the sites mentioned are base camps from which foraging for food and hunting would have taken place. Very few structures, which might be termed dwellings, from this period have been found but hearths are common on most sites and, although tent-like structures would leave little trace, it is likely that tents made of animal skins sewn together were the normal form of house. Modern nomads use similar tents which are easily collapsible.

At most sites which have been excavated there are remnants of stake holes and post holes, but it is difficult to interpret these as anything more than tent-like structures. At one site, Broom Hill, Braishfield, near Romsey in Hampshire a series of post and stake holes surrounds an artificial hollow in which there was a central post and internal hearth; this is one of the most convincing Mesolithic houses ever to be found (**19**).

The reconstruction (**colour plate 3**) summarises much of what is known about the Mesolithic settlements. A small group of tents and associated structure for drying fish and hides would have been situated in a forest clearance with easy access for water. The bow and arrow was an essential everyday weapon and wood working (centre foreground) an important task for making arrows and boats (middle right). Deer, birds and the sea also played an important part in early post-glacial life. John Wymer in his Shire Archaeology publication on Mesolithic Britain paints a posi-

tive picture of life in a Mesolithic settlement. 'The camp would have been a busy place, when fully occupied, with old equipment being repaired and new being made. Ethnographic parallels suggest that the people would have entertained themselves with story-telling, music, singing and dancing.' We know very little about their customs (marriage ceremonies, birth and death rituals).

In the Test Valley in Hampshire, a Mesolithic site, Bowmans Farm, (excavated in ten days because of the pressure of the pipeline construction), was situated on the edge of the flood plain of the River Blackwater (**20**). The flint from the site is late Mesolithic or even transitional Neolithic. A preliminary radiocarbon date of 4800 BC fits in well with the lithic material.

The four houses found during top-soil clearing constituted two pairs of shallow ring ditches, one pair 25m (82ft) apart and the other 10m (32ft) apart. The ring slots were filled with large quantities of charcoal. The entrances were to the south-south-east and the fourth house was more sub-rectangular than circular. The topsoil was only 30cm (1ft) in depth and had it been ploughed regularly then it would have been destroyed (and was not likely to have shown as a crop mark). Wood from the site has been identified as oak, willow, poplar, birch, and buckthorn; hazel is attested from the nuts found. These species would have provided adequate building material for post and wattles. From the analysis of the carbonised deposits there is some evidence for seasonal activity.

The discovery of this highlights how new material can be brought to light; the local Sites and Monuments Record (SMR) was asked for information in this area and it was shown to be 'archaeologically blank'; given currently available information the pipeline in this area did not seem to be damaging any archaeology. Fortunately the whole length of the pipeline was archaeologically evaluated once the topsoil had been stripped (as fieldwalking would have revealed little). It was during the topsoil strip-

19 *Broomhill, one of the few structures from the Mesolithic period* (after Wymer).

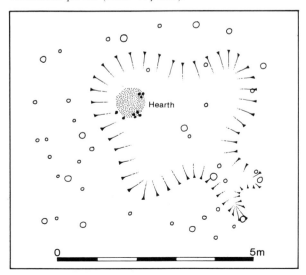

Hearth

0   5m

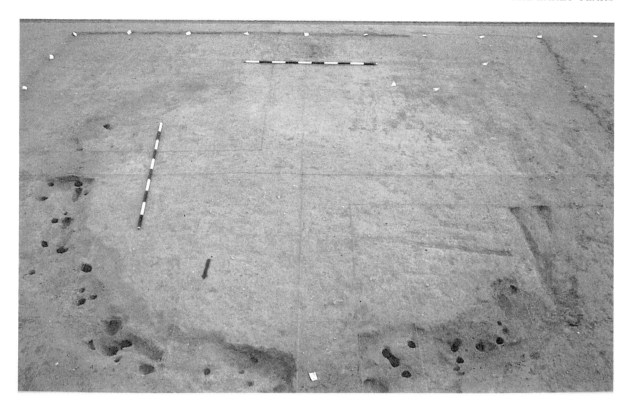

20 *Bowman's Farm settlement, Hampshire. House 3 after excavation* (photograph copyright of Test Valley Archaeological Trust).

ping that the site was found

It is worth stressing that the information contained within any recording system is the current state of knowledge and not confirmation of the presence or absence of sites; surveys and evaluations have to be done continuously if we are not to lose unrecorded archaeological information.

If this hunter-gatherer way of life was so successful why did it change? Why should these communities change from semi-mobile groups with a good resource base and develop farming practices? Was it population pressure/growth, was it external contacts? It is now well-established that farming (growing crops and husbanding livestock) spread from the Near East, where the wild progenitors of the cereal plants lived, which were to form the basis of the new

economy (**21**). The causes (and effects) of the spread of farming have been the subject of many books and there is one fundamental point worthy of discussion, which has changed over the past 20 years. When the spread of farming had become understood as a phenomenon, theories about the changes it brought were developed. Initially it was argued that farming produced sedentary population and 'surplus labour' and therefore there was the possibility for building large monuments (henges, long barrows, causewayed camps, stone circles and avenues, for example). However, anthropological research was also beginning to show that the first affluent societies were hunter-gatherers or foragers; they had time on their hands too, if even they were supposedly 'mobile' populations. More recently the opposite argument is being made that it was the building of the monuments, by semi-mobile populations, which brought about a social change and it was as a result of the monument building that

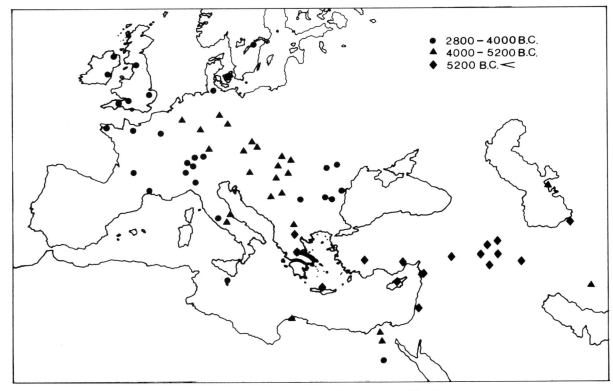

21 *The spread of farming into Europe* (after Clark).

these populations took up farming and 'settled' in purpose-built settlements.

Whatever the answer, change did take place, but how did it manifest in terms of human settlement?

By the end of the fifth millennium the population was becoming larger and forming tribes (probably) with exchange mechanisms. Then in the fourth millennium the pace of changes accelerated with the introduction of agriculture. Not surprisingly this had a profound affect on the landscape and on 'prehistoric settlements'. It is possible that the effect of the arrival of farming has been overstated, especially in the Neolithic and Bronze Age. Ideas and models about pastoralism and pastoralists are in the doldrums and much of archaeological thought and theory is often as a result of modern intellectual fashion (currently involving structuralism, post-Modernism, processual and post-processual archaeology); but

pastoralism is perhaps staging a comeback as more evidence comes to light of a combination of herding and crop cultivation from the Neolithic onwards.

In the Mesolithic – or the 'bit after the glaciers but before farming' – it is easier to talk about individual sites (as there are relatively few of them) and at the same time begin to understand something of the changing landscape of the time.

However, the changes in the landscape are not reflected by changes in technology. Similarly a change in technology does not necessarily herald a change in economy, land-use, or settlement pattern. There are many other forces at work which will have affected the decision-making of prehistoric farmers. In terms of understanding prehistoric settlement through time it is instructive to look at a number of landscapes and see how they were used from the Neolithic to the end of the Iron Age.

4

Early Farmers and Neolithic Settlement

Towards the end of the fifth millennium BC a combination of factors lead to the adoption of farming and a reduction in the hunter-gatherer way of life. For a considerable period of time, into the second millennium BC, and in some places even into the first millennium BC, prehistoric communities in the British Isles did not rely solely on farming; with abundant natural resources there was no need to. The adoption of farming techniques and processes took place at different places and at different rates during the fifth and fourth millennia (from about 4300 to 3500 BC).

The transition from hunter-gatherer to farmer took place over a large area (from the Near-East to Britain, from Northern Europe to the Mediterranean) and not all at one time (**21**). Detecting the transition in the archaeological record is virtually impossible; gradually we see indicators of a more settled way of life, with the construction of large monuments which have survived several thousand years. This so-called 'Neolithic Revolution' is more of a transition than revolution in the modern sense of the word. There can be no doubt that the former hunter-gatherer way of life had been overturned but it did not happen overnight and the evidence from early Neolithic Britain suggests a combination of settled farming with a mixture of hunting and gathering. The crucial point is how does this change manifest itself in the archaeological record in terms of settlement sites?

This is difficult to answer if we are looking for villages, or hamlets of Neolithic farmers. I would suggest we need to approach the subject in terms of understanding the way in which Neolithic people used their landscape; if we do that then we can place the sites we know to be Neolithic in an understandable context.

There are many examples to choose from and I will take the Somerset Levels as an example of the way in which one type of landscape was used. Having done this the picture will be broadened to include 'causewayed camps', and then a few known Neolithic settlements from Orkney to Cornwall; finally the evidence we have for individual houses will be looked at.

The wets and wood

The story of the Somerset Levels in prehistory and the way in which sites were discovered has been fully told in *Sweet Track to Glastonbury*, by John Coles and Bryony Coles published in 1986. The reader is urged to consult this book for a greater understanding of the way in which prehistorians can provide answers to the fundamental questions of who was living when and where.

The authors of that book freely admit that they do not know where all the people lived, or what the size of the settlements were (although other areas help us to answer these questions). However, by using the evidence from the Sweet Track, a Neolithic trackway across a watery,

22 *The Sweet Track, a wooden trackway 5800 years old* (Somerset Levels Project).

From the evidence of woodland management these groups had been living in the area for at least a generation; the hazel tree-ring evidence points to this, as does the fact that some of the ash used in the Sweet Track had been felled at least 30 years before the track was constructed. The people using the trackways stayed for about 10 years; the track was repaired for up to 10 years after it had been built. The track became engulfed in the peat during the third millennium which has preserved it for the past 5000 years.

Normally we would label the people living in and around the Somerset Levels (and other

23 *A reconstruction of the Meare Heath bow, made of yew with probable decorative binding* (Somerset Levels Project, drawn by M. Rouillard).

boggy area of what is now a peat area, we can deduce the following facts about the Neolithic people (**22**).

The wood for the trackway can be seen to have to have been felled in one single year, in the winter of 3806/7 BC. (This is an absolute date, based on dendrochronology.) The conversion of the trunks into planks must have taken place immediately as the roundwood (for pegs and rails) was cut to length and sharpened before it was seasoned. It has been estimated that enough wood was prepared for 6000 pegs, 2000 metres of rails and 400 metres of planking. The species of wood (over a dozen) were from two different woodlands, one in the north and one to the south. It has been suggested that this represented two families (or groups of adults) working at two locations. We can therefore suggest at least two settlements, one to the north and one to the south of the low-lying areas.

similar areas) 'farmers', but we must not think of them as farmers in the modern sense of the word. They 'farmed' some parts of the land, and were probably more settled than the communities living 500 or more years before. The evidence for them being farmers is slight indeed, and with the natural resources which the Levels would have provided the need for farming was not great. Why grow crops when you can obtain a plentiful supply (and variety) of food from the back garden? There is some pollen evidence from the Westhay area to suggest that some cereal was grown and that the forests were cleared. It is not absolutely certain that the builders of the trackways were farmers. They were hunters as the Meare Heath bow shows (**23**). They were also affluent (by Neolithic standards), leaving fine pottery behind and one finely made jadeite axe. These artefacts also suggest that they had good external contacts; perhaps indicative of a highly mobile society which had its base around the Levels.

The Sweet Track (named after Ray Sweet, the local person who discovered it) is not unique. There are many more tracks; another one being Garvin's brushwood track built about 2400 BC (or 3000 BC after calibration).

One feature of Neolithic society was its mobility and the differences from region to region. It is perhaps in the nature of our own society that we want to understand 'cultures' or 'society' as some sort of homogeneous entity. This is to impose our twentieth-century ideas and cultural thinking on a population which thrived 5000 years ago.

The settlements of the builders of the Sweet Track and Garvin's brushwood track in the Somerset Levels may well have been hamlets with houses made of wood; we know they were skilled carpenters. Yet, if the settlements were located on the higher, drier ground to the north and south, the wood would not have survived and we have to remain thankful that the last trace of their manipulation of the area, the trackways, have survived.

In other parts of the country we have not

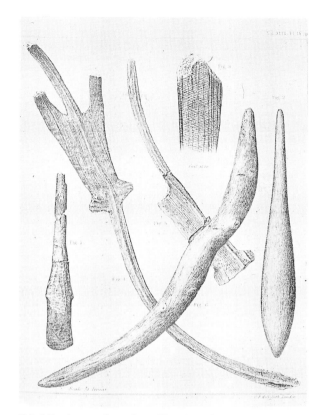

24 *Wooden artefacts from Ehenside Tarn, Cumbria.*

been so lucky, but a rare example of a Neolithic settlement is Ehenside Tarn, Cumbria discovered and 'excavated' in the 1870s; the artefacts which were discovered there (**24**) are still some of the finest wooden objects from the Neolithic times. This site consisted of a series of hearths around what must have been a lake or tarn (cf. Barfield Tarn). The tarn had filled up and become a peat-bog which the farmer decided to drain in 1869. During these drainage works a number of Neolithic polished stone axes and wooden artefacts were discovered (**24**). This site still represents the best Neolithic site in the area in terms of preservation; yet it can only have been a settlement for one or two families. The evidence for a large Neolithic population in the area is based on finds of Group VI axes (from Langdale, see **colour plate 4**). The distribution of stone axes throughout the area was interesting but not indicative of a large settled popu-

25 *Plasketlands, Cumbria. A Neolithic site discovered by aerial photography and excavated by the author* (Crown Copyright).

lation. The axes which have been found and recorded were either from the small glacial ridges which are a common feature in the area (up to 25m (76ft) above OD) or were found near bogs or tarns. A distribution of the bogs in the area taken from the 1st Edition Ordnance Survey map, has over 30 bogs in 700 sq. miles (1800 sq.km), which shows that mobile groups would have a plentiful supply of fish, birds and game which would inhabit these areas. Given the proximity of the sea, marine resources were important throughout the Mesolithic and no doubt the Neolithic as well.

Similar to the use of the Brue valley in the Somerset Levels these Neolithic people were using the local resources for their food supply, as much if not more, than farming. The settlement pattern for this area of Cumbria, the Solway Plain, was likely to have been small groups of highly mobile people moving through the area and beyond; perhaps stationary for a summer or two but certainly not sedentary and chopping down trees (particularly elm) as clearance areas for their farms.

Interestingly one site, a D-shaped enclosure showing only as a crop-mark site, was excavated and, despite an expected Iron Age date, produced three Neolithic radiocarbon dates, which when calibrated are early Neolithic c. 3400 BC (**8, 25**). The function of this site is, however, unknown but its construction used large timbers, probably oak; so far it too is unique in the area. It can be argued that the location of any site is important in terms of its 'catchment', or territory. This has led to a large body of literature on 'site catchment analysis' and I maintain that this site, Plasketlands, is a settlement. Its proximity to the sea, as mentioned above, has to be set alongside the sandy soils and fertile (high and dry) position.

The elm decline

Relevant here is a discussion of the cause of the 'elm decline' at c. 3000 BC. This is a good example of the way ideas change within a generation as well as being a watershed in prehistory. Pollen studies began to show throughout Europe that at about 3000 bc there was a definite decline in one particular tree, elm. One study in 1966 argued strongly for an anthropogenic (man-made) cause for the elm-decline in northern Cumbria. If this was the case there should be good evidence for the Neolithic settlements in the area. To affect the tree population to the extent that it can be recorded in the remains of tree pollen is no mean feat. So, where were all the Neolithic sites? Is the elm decline man-made or does it have another cause? The recent elm decline which was caused by an elm disease (a microscopic fungus, *Ceratocystis ulmi*) which is transmitted by two bark beetles (*Scolytus scolytus* and *S. multistriatus*). In the light of this, Oliver Rackham has proposed an interesting alternative cause to the elm decline. The elm species has been subject to a series of declines since records began and he postulates that the bettle which transmits the disease could have been active as long ago as the Neolithic and it is partly coincidental with the expansion during the Neolithic that the decline took place c. 3000 BC.

A further argument against an anthropogenic cause is that it is elm which declines more than any other species; if prehistoric communities were clearing woodland, or managing woodland, this clearance would not be so species-specific. This is despite the theory that in Denmark cattle were fed on elm leaves,

and therefore their use as fodder aided their decline; this is a questionable proposition on the grounds that the population of cattle to consume these leaves would have been enormous *and* the human population needed to eat the cattle would also have been far greater than all estimates suggest. Also, if elm trees are your main source of food for cattle, you would surely wish to maintain them and not let them decline.

This discussion is relevant in that it highlights the interrelated nature of many disciplines which aid archaeologists in their interpretations. Archaeology has to seek assistance from other sciences to corroborate, or refute, the information it derives from survey and excavation. A good example of this is the evidence from bettle remains found in samples of peat taken from around the Sweet Track. Five of the species identified are no longer found in Britain and four may have become extinct (in Britain) because of climatic change. When the distribution of these four (*Ooedes gracilis*, *Chlaenius sulcicolis*, *Anthicus gracilis*, and *Airaphilus elongatus*) was examined it showed that they favoured a more continental climate perhaps with winters 2–4°C colder and summers 2–3°C warmer.

Causewayed camps

Let us now turn from landscapes where Neolithic populations were known to have settled but for which details of individual settlements is limited, and concentrate on the beginnings of 'enclosures'.

There is a type of site known as causewayed camps; it could be argued these sites have no place in a book on prehistoric settlements but they are too important as a group to leave out when we know so little about their function, and they represent some of the first enclosing activities in the archaeological record.

Any 'enclosing' is a fundamental, social, intellectual and political move that is irreversible. It is also seen first in the interrupted ditches of causewayed camps. Causewayed camps are not in any way confining, given their size, 1.7–

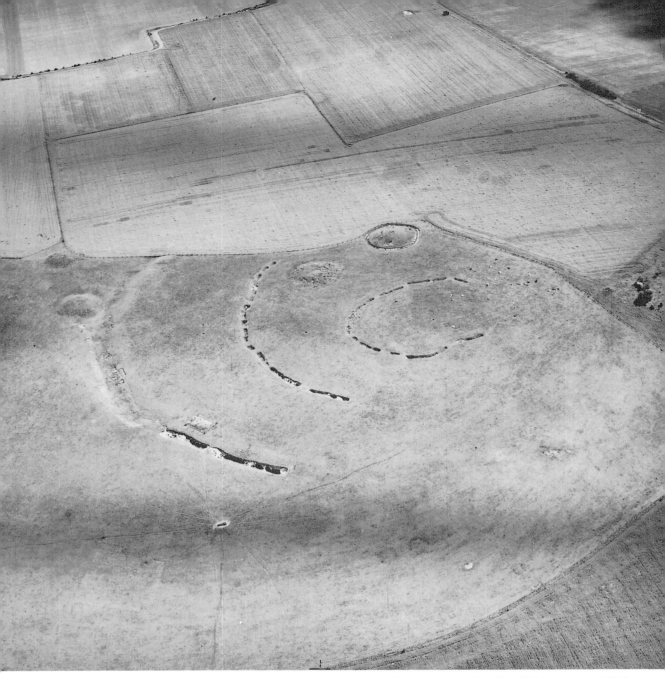

9.6ha (4.2–23.7 acres); but they do represent the first formal enclosure for communal activity. We cannot fit them into a single category – are they settlements, ritual, or burial sites? They are all these and we should try to understand how they operated in Neolithic society. If they are not settlements then they performed an important function as part of the Neolithic landscape and undoubtedly cut across the boundaries between domestic, economic and ritual behaviour which have been so compartmentalised in today's society.

As a class of site they are one feature of the Neolithic landscape which was not a long barrow, henge, passage grave or monument connected with the burial ritual. Archaeologists have to use labels and names: the 'causewayed camp' is so-called because of the encircling ditches having causeways at regular intervals. In the low-lying areas of Britain this type of site has been referred to as an 'interrupted ditch system' (i.d.s. for short). Here I will use the term causewayed camp to include all sites, whether earthworks or crop marks, which have an encircling ditch with causeways within it (**26** and **colour plate 1**). Rog Palmer has shown that there are two 'groups' of causewayed camp – those which mainly survive as earthworks with widely spaced ditches, either single or multiple ditches, and all on high or hill-top locations. The other group, by contrast,

are low-lying, with closely spaced ditches, perhaps more defensive, and usually on sloping ground near rivers (**27**). This may relate to the function of the sites or it may be that the sites perform a similar function in different locations and it is the location which determines the form of the site. A visit to Windmill Hill is instructive in that it does not look like a hill until you are standing on top of it (**26**).

Further analysis of the camps by Palmer divides them into four groups (Midlands, Thames, Southwest, Sussex) and into two size categories; the smaller from 1.7 to 3.5ha (4.2–8.6 acres), and the larger 5.5 to 9.6ha (13.5–28 acres). Groupings were attempted in a variety of ways. Geographical location was a strong indicator but other methods

27 *Four possible groups of Neolithic interrupted ditch systems* (after R. Palmer).

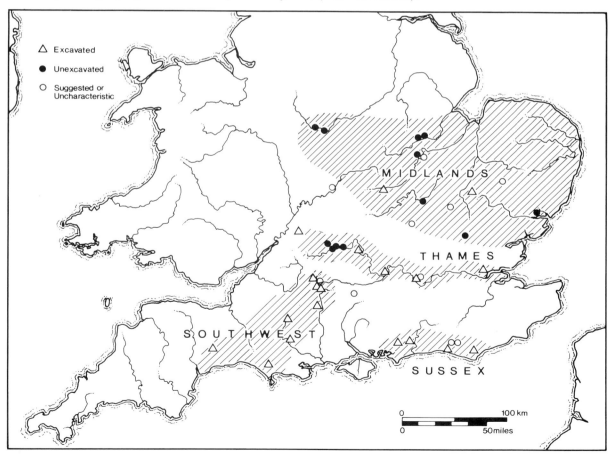

were also employed, such as classifying the sites according to the number and spacing of the enclosing ditches (**27**).

Figure **28** shows a southern England distribution of 64 sites, none north of a line from the Humber to the south-west through Staffordshire. This is not an accident of discovery as there have been many years of searching (through aerial photography and other techniques) throughout Britain. It is possible further research will widen this distribution.

Another way of grouping these sites has been by examining the pottery styles in the Neolithic. Roger Mercer argues that the pottery styles can be seen to be cultural and that the distribution of pottery production can be divided

28 *The distribution of causewayed camps in England (after Mercer). 1 Carn Brea; 2 Helman Tor; 3 High Peak; 4 Hembury; 5 Membury; 6 Maiden Castle; 7 Hambledon Hill; 8 Whitesheet Hill; 9 Robin Hood's Ball; 10 Rybury; 11 Windmill Hill; 12 Overton Hill; 13 Knap Hill; 14 Crofton; 15 Beacon Hill; 16 The Trundle; 17 Bury Hill; 18 Barkhale; 19 Whitehawk; 20 Court Hill; 21 Offham Hill; 22 Malling Hill; 23 Combe Hill; 24 Chalk; 25 Orsett; 26 East Bedfont; 27 Staines; 28 Eton Wick; 29 Dorney Reach; 30 Dunsden; 31 Blewburton Hill; 32 Abingdon; 33 Aston; 34 Broadwell; 35 Langford; 36 Down Ampney; 37 Eastleach; 38 Signet Hill; 39 Icomb Hill; 40 Southmoor; 41 Crickley Hill; 42 The Peak; 43 Sawbridgeworth; 44 Maiden Bower; 45 Freston; 46 Fornham All Saints; 47 Great Wilbraham; 48 Melbourn; 49 Cardington; 50 Briar Hill; 51 Dallington Heath; 52 Hampton Lucy; 53 Haddenham; 54 Tansor; 55 Southwick; 56 Etton; 57 Barholm; 58 Uffington; 59 Hainford; 60 Roughton; 61 Alrewas; 62 Mavesyn Ridware; 63 South Kirkby; 64 Buckland.*

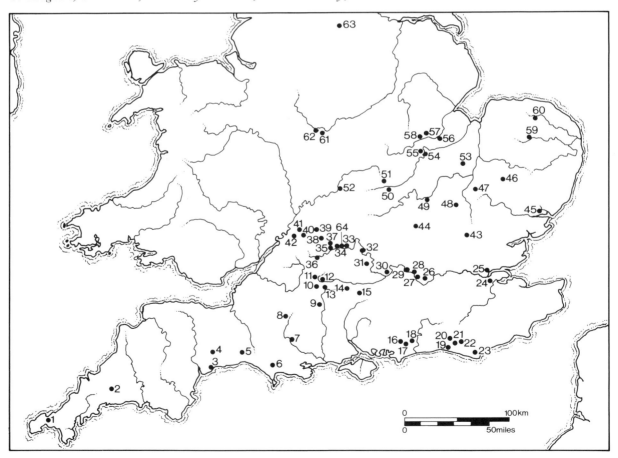

into four: (i) a south-west group including Cornwall, Devon, Dorset; (ii) a Wessex and west to the Cotswolds group; (iii) a Sussex group; (iv) a central group in the Thames Valley, the Chilterns, East Anglia and the east and central midlands. (There is a fifth group, the northern Grimston-Lyles Hill group, outside the distribution of causewayed camps.) The distribution of these pottery styles is in certain cases coincident with the distribution of causewayed camps. More work is needed on this but it is a beginning in terms of groupings, especially if combined with Palmer's proposed groupings.

The proposal that a particular pottery style is equal to a particular 'cultural group' is questionable but is commonly argued in archaeology. Linking four pottery styles with the tentative results of the four 'causewayed camp groups' is stretching the evidence to the limit. It does, however, produce a hypothesis for further work. It introduces for the first time in prehistoric communities in Britain the suggestion that the population was sufficiently large to have allowed for regional variation and diversity; indeed, as will be shown below, there is strong evidence for conflict between these groups.

The history of causewayed camp studies is interesting from the point of view demonstrating how archaeologists work and how the subject is always changing. First of all a site – or a number of sites – is discovered, and then a label is given to one of them – in the 1680s the classic causewayed camp, Windmill Hill (**26**), was referred to as a Roman Camp. Then there is a period of more survey, excavations and research and a 'class' of site emerges, in this case 'causewayed camp'; as early as the 1930s Neolithic camps were defined as having certain characteristics; causeways, concentric lines of defence where necessary, following the contour, and situated on prominent hills and ridges. As time has passed many of the sites included in the class have been excluded, so the 'class' is always redefining itself; the need

for this is increased by new discoveries, either through fieldwork or more often through aerial photography (**colour plate 1**).

We cannot use modern divisions of function and causewayed camps could be schools, banks, stock exchanges (in the original sense of the term), law courts, barracks, hospitals, and homes. It is also worth noting that not all Neolithic enclosures are causewayed (Court Hill, Singleton and Bury Hill, Houghton).

The function of one causewayed camp, Hambledon Hill (**29**), has been argued for after extensive excavation. As we have seen the act of 'enclosing' was an important development in human history and Roger Mercer argues that this represents a farming economy dominated by cattle herding. Cattle can be seen as a mobile source of wealth which is in need of

29 *Hambledon Hill from the air showing the Iron Age hillfort with earlier long barrows inside it (middle right) and the causewayed camp with the remains of excavations visible as a white patch (middle) and the Stepleton enclosure, which is possibly a Neolithic settlement (top left)* (Cambridge University Collection of Air Photographs: copyright reserved).

protection, as well as being kept out of the settlements. If they are a source of wealth they will be coveted by others and in Mercer's words they play a part 'in stimulating easily satisifed greed, feed the notion of intercommunal conflict. Enclosure is a response to these demands.' Hambledon Hill contains a number of enclosures; the earliest is the Stepleton enclosure, which encloses about 1ha (2.4 acres). The evidence that this enclosure was a settlement, some of which had been removed by subsequent use of the hill-top, comes from pits with domestic rubbish, broken flint tools, fragments of eroded pottery, fragments of animal bone and carbonised vegetable matter. Included in the organic remains were remnants of emmer, einkorn, barley and one seed of *Vitis vinifera*, domesticated grape, unique in the British Neolithic; was it a long-distance import? There is also evidence of an oven, flint and antler workings, plus the remains of a still-born child in the cavity of the wall. All these finds suggest that domestic activity was an important part of the function of the site. However, the bone assemblage suggests feasting rather than careful meat management. Whole articulated joints of meat were partially consumed and then discarded.

Whatever the nature of activity here, the defences were enlarged and the top people wanted to remain on top. There was evidence of a conflagration – the recently cut ditches of the larger site were open and clean when fire swept through the site; the wind appears to have been in the north-west and the timber of the rampart burnt and fell into the ditches. Beneath one part of the rampart, which had collapsed into the ditch, two skeletons were found of men aged 20. One had been shot in the back by an arrow while carrying a young child; he had either fallen or been pushed and this action caused the child to be crushed or at best smothered. The other man had at least been buried but his grave had been back-filled with scorched chalk, probably derived from the rampart debris.

There was obviously a need for defence but why enclose such a large area? The answer may be gained from the animal bone evidence – Tony Legge examined the bone from Hambledon Hill and concluded that the herd was predominantly for milk production with a certain number of cattle reserved for meat consumption. Yet there is no water, so any protection within the enclosure was surely for short-term expediency.

The construction of the defences in their final phase may seem a massive investment in labour to counter raids or short-lived warfare; yet it was designed to protect the main food resource. Hambledon Hill itself encloses over 50ha (123 acres) with partial defences, with a timber-reinforced rampart which was later added to by a double line of outer defences: there were three timber-lined gateways and it has been estimated that over 10,000 timbers were used in the construction of the defences. All of this immense defensive work had been constructed by 2700 BC. This was a huge investment of labour probably for cattle herding, but the lack of water suggests, at least to the excavator, that the site would not have withstood a long siege and that the substantial defences, therefore, were as much a symbol of power as an effective refuge. The evidence suggests that the site was used as a settlement, as the hill-top was used for many centuries.

A site which has been compared with the early phase of Hambledon Hill is Carn Brea, south-west of Redruth in Cornwall. The defences of this site encircle two summits and an area of 18ha (46 acres) with two smaller enclosures around the central and eastern summits. The eastern enclosure contains good settlement evidence, and encloses about 1ha (2.4 acres); its wall is made of massive rocks weighing up to 3 tonnes and joins naturally defensive rocks. Within the enclosure are a number of terraces on which timber houses were built, probably enough for 100–150 people. Apart from the obvious activities of obtaining food through farming (and no doubt cattle played an important part in this), the people were involved in a number of economic activities.

At this time (c. 3000–2700 BC) the production of polished stone axes was a major industry (not just in Cornwall but throughout Britain); at Carn Brea large amounts of the stone from the Camborne area (Group XVI rock) was worked and polished for the 'trade' in stone axes. The exact mechanics of the trade have not been possible to work out, but it is likely that causewayed camps, large enclosures and henges were important meeting places, even markets for these sorts of goods. This activity gave the inhabitants of Carn Brea a certain power and status. They were able to import pottery from over 30km (19 miles) away and the chert (a type of flint) from Devon and Dorset. The problem with any power base is that at some point it has to be defended and sustained. The evidence from Carn Brea was that it was attacked from all sides by archers (over 800 arrowheads have been found); the walls were slighted and there is evidence of universal burning across the site. The site was not, as far as the excavator can tell, ever re-occupied in the Neolithic. What the cause of this attack was we will never know, but it does highlight the beginning of the tensions between communities once territories and locations are marked out as belonging to one group.

The axe trade also brings us to a site near Honiton in Devon, Hembury, which has Neolithic origins and suffered a similar fate as Carn Brea. Hembury occupies a promontory site and was also occupied in the Iron Age. In the Neolithic the evidence from excavations in the 1930s suggests that the site had been attacked; the ditches had been filled with a mass of burnt material leaving a layer of charcoal no less than 15cm (6in) thick and in places up to 60cm (2ft) thick. In amongst this burnt debris were 120 leaf-shaped arrowheads. Prior to its destruction Hembury had been part of a trade network which imported gabbro-gritted pottery from south-west Cornwall, as well as a trade in flint

and chert (from Dorset) and stone axes from Cornwall.

Another site where similar events took place is at Crickley Hill, near Cheltenham in Gloucestershire; the first occupation on this site was of an oval barrow, but with no burial. The area was subsequently cleared and the ditch of a causewayed camp excavated; within the enclosure rectangular houses were found ranging in size from 5 × 2m (15 × 6ft) to 10 × 5m (30 × 15ft). It seems that this site too, had been attacked by archers. Crickley Hill also attracts attention because of the discovery of what appears to be a 'shrine' – a stone built platform, the centre of which was kept clean, even though the area around contained 'midden debris'. It is associated with an orthostat. The shrine appears to have been in use long after the site, as a settlement or defensive refuge had been abandoned.

One aspect of Neolithic sites, causewayed camps in particular, which can be detected throughout prehistory is the tradition of continuity – at least three sites, Hembury, Maiden Castle and the Trundle, hill tops were used as causewayed camps in the Neolithic and were also used as major strategic defences in the Iron Age.

By contrast, another well-known but recently discovered and excavated site is Etton, near Peterborough. Its situation is low-lying by contrast with the sites mentioned above. The site was discovered during the hot summer of 1976 by aerial photography and showed as a very faint crop mark (**30**). The reason for this was that the archaeological features were buried beneath almost a metre of alluvium which had built up over 5000 years in the Welland valley. Important to the excavations carried out by Francis Pryor and his team was the discovery of the waterlogged deposits on the site; this has added an enormous amount of information about this type of site, without providing us with any clearer answers! The ditches enclosing the site were cut into the gravel and the material from the ditch spread

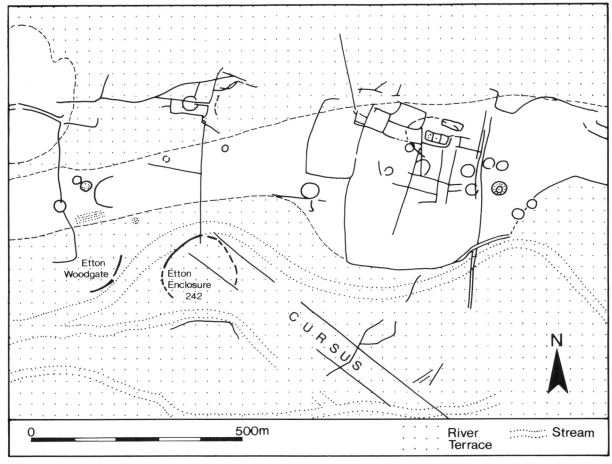

30 *Plan of the causewayed camp at Etton* (after Pryor).

across the interior of the site; there appears to have been no attempt to build a rampart. There were causeways between the ditches. The ditches seems to have been open for a relatively short time and were re-cut a total of eight times, probably on a seasonal basis. There is evidence of at least one rectangular structure in the interior.

The results of environmental analysis indicate that cereal was being grown and that cattle were once again a dominant part of the economy. Any attempt at reconstructing the way of life of the people as part-time cereal producers with seasonally grazing cattle has to include the 'ritual' aspect of life at the time.

Deposits which are not connected with what we know of domestic life have been found. In one ditch terminal there was a deliberate deposit which contained a neatly arranged bundle of meat (only the bone survives), with calf bones and a complete Mildenhall ware bowl. All these were placed on a birch-bark mat. Another section of ditch appears to have been deliberately back-filled with 'deposits' placed within and beneath the back-filling. For example, cremated human bone was placed next to a human skull with an antler 'baton' and a small standing stone nearby. A wooden vessel was also placed near this collection of artefacts. These deposits were obviously important to the people making them and may have had some apotropaic function, but we can only speculate on their significance.

These sites and discoveries highlight on the one hand how little we know of the nature of Neolithic settlement, and on the other the variety and complexity of society 5000 years ago. There are many ritual aspects to these sites; to have excluded them would have been to reinforce our own concepts of what is domestic, economic, and ritual or spiritual. Any distinction between these aspects of life is a false one as we all have everyday rituals, which may be mundane but which to the archaeologist or anthropologist may have some significance.

If we cast our net slightly wider for a moment and look at Neolithic towns, even cities, in Turkey the combination of home and shrine, or Do-it-yourself divinity is evident. At Çatal Huyuk in Anatolia there is a Neolithic mud-brick town and the rectangular houses (with a floor area of about 25 sq. m, 135 sq. ft) are interspersed with shrines in considerable numbers; although the shrines themselves are special places. Throughout history this is not an uncommon practice: the Romans had household gods and shrines as well as external temples.

The Orkneys

Recent work on the Neolithic sites in Orkney has shown the importance of design and layout on Neolithic settlements. At two sites Skara Brae and Barnhouse, settlements of stone houses have survived very well. The Orkney islands have preserved whole landscapes of prehistoric life and nowhere is the evidence for a Neolithic village better preserved.

The story of Skara Brae has been told on many occasions, and like so many Neolithic sites its end was catastrophic (**31**). In this instance it was a natural disaster, probably due

31 *Skara Brae, Orkney. A Neolithic stone built settlement, abandoned after a storm* (Crown Copyright: Royal Commission on the Ancient and Historical Monuments of Scotland).

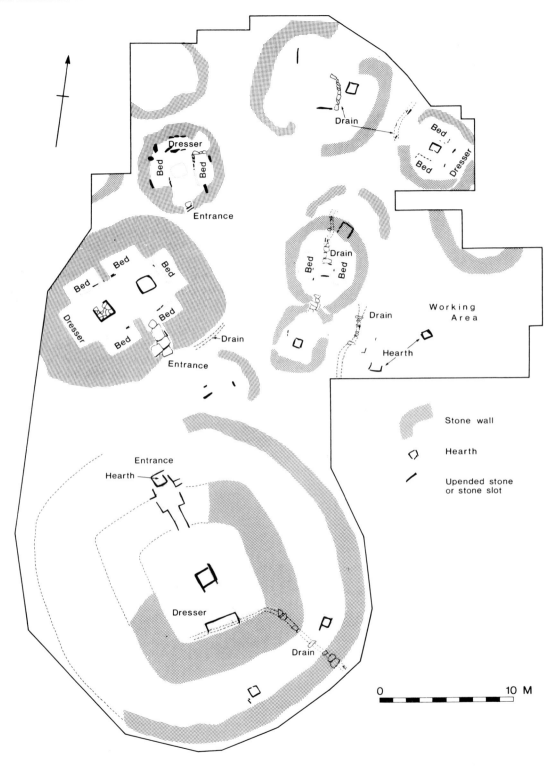

Stone wall

Hearth

Upended stone
or stone slot

0   10 M

32 *Plan of the Neolithic settlement at Barnhouse, Orkney* (courtesy of C. Richards).

to a massive storm which swamped the site in sea and sand. This natural act also allowed its preservation for 50 centuries. The site was discovered to the modern world in 1850 and has been subject to excavation six times, the first systematic excavation was undertaken by Professor Gordon Childe in 1927. The site was occupied for a number of generations (perhaps 20–25) as there is evidence of at least four building phases. Its maximum size was achieved with eight stone built houses (all with interconnecting passages) with a population of about 50. Each house has an entrance, a rectangular hearth and stone recesses, dressers and stone 'box' beds for sleeping; only one house had a window and all these features are stone-built. The roof may have been supported by whale bones.

The coastal setting is a familiar prehistoric one and the excavations of the midden deposits show that the marine resources were well used, especially limpets (there is a suggestion that the limpets were used as fish-bait). Bones from wild (red deer) and domesticated animals (cow and sheep) were also discovered, including birds and fish. Burnt grain was also found; evidence that the combination of crops, cattle rearing and natural resources enabled the community to survive at Skara Brae for nearly 1000 years (3200–220 BC). The occupants were also skilled craftsmen making elaborately decorated tools, weapons and ornaments; there is also a suggestion that they painted themselves with red paint as small containers which contained red ochre have been found.

Another site in Orkney, recently discovered, is that of Barnhouse (**32**), a late Neolithic settlement, near the Stones of Stenness. The original village was constructed around 3200 BC and it is different from the village of Skara Brae. The largest house, no. 2 on the plan, is symmetrical on the axis of the doorway with six recesses (reminiscent of the burial chamber at Maeshowe, which is in view of Barnhouse today). The house had two large and elaborately constructed hearths centrally placed. The

architecture of the house is similar to the passage tomb of Maeshowe and a further connection is a burial, in a stone cist (covered by a flagstone) in the south-west portion of the house. A further 15 houses were excavated and these other houses were of a different construction, being circular in shape and probably having turf roofs and comparable to many other Neolithic houses on Orkney.

The standard architecture for a Neolithic house in Orkney is the 'dresser' opposite the entrance with stone-box beds on the right and left of a stone-built hearth. As Colin Richards, the excavator at Barnhouse, points out, the hearth may not have been centrally located but it did play a central role in Orcadian life; this was as true in the Neolithic as it is today. The central stone hearth has a stone box bed to the right and left, and it has been suggested that the larger right-hand bed might have been male and the smaller left-hand bed female. Richards argues that the hearth is not just the centre of the house but the centre of the Neolithic world, the *axis mundi*, which provides an eternal reference point from which everything and everyone takes their position and orientation. It provides fire and light, two essential prerequisites for life in Orkney. Keeping the fire going, and never letting it go out was an important symbol of unity and well being. The Neolithic stone hearth can be seen to have been the focal point around which the house was built.

Three further elements of the site must be noted. The circular houses were demolished and replaced whereas house 2 remained in use throughout the history of the settlement. An area to the east of house 2 in the centre of the settlement was where pottery manufacture, stone working, bone and flint working took place (in the open area between houses 6, 7 and 12). Finally, the largest stone-built feature on the site, no. 8 on the plan, requires some explanation (**32**). This construction consists of a outer enclosing wall, 1.5m (4.5ft) thick and over 25m (78ft) in diameter; inside it a house-like building, with a 7 × 7m (22 × 22ft) inner floor area with a large central hearth and a rear dresser, was encased in the 3m (10ft) thick wall. A complete Grooved ware vessel was set into the floor near the eastern wall. The entrance faces north-west, the direction of the setting midsummer sun and included a monumental porch construction. This building is the latest on the site, as it overlies earlier features and is therefore a Neolithic monument in its own right. Its exact role is open to speculation, but once again we can see the inextricable connection between domestic and ritual activity.

Other sites in lowland Britain and Ireland

The evidence for Neolithic settlement in other parts of Britain is patchy; there are examples at places like Fengate and Balleygalley in N. Ireland of rectangular houses and their associations are interesting (**33**). Both have artefacts from the Langdale axe factory (**colour plate 4**) and the long-distance trade of material for axes throughout Britain has been studied in great detail by the Implement Petrology Research Group.

The Fengate house was excavated in 1972 on the Padholme Road site in the Fengate area of Peterborough. The house measures 7 × 18.5m (22 × 26ft). The walls were of wattle covered with untempered clay based on a wooden frame. The roof was probably of thatch. A corner post gave a radiocarbon date of 2445 BC, and it probably housed four to six people. In the ditches of the house a number of flint artefacts were found, but the most interesting finds were a fragment of a polished stone axe from the Langdale axe factory, Cumbria (**colour plate 4**) and a jet bead; the major source for the latter is in north Yorkshire. This

33 *Neolithic house at Balleygalley, Northern Ireland* (courtesy of D. Simpson).

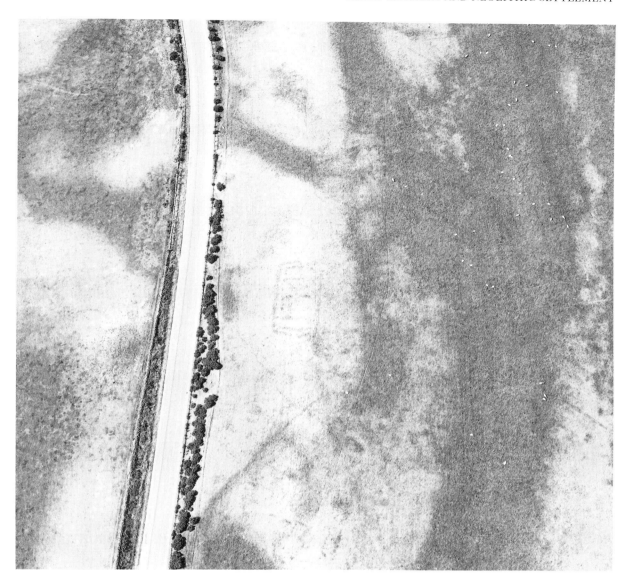

34 *Crop marks of a Neolithic house at Balbridie, Scotland* (Crown Copyright: Royal Commission on the Ancient and Historical Monuments of Scotland).

is further evidence for long-distance trade, either by a series of networks or individuals travelling long distances.

More recently the excavations at Balley-galley, on the north-east coast of Ireland have revealed a house; the walls of the house would have been wooden planks laid in the slot trench with an internal double row of post-holes (**33**). This rectangular house had been deliberately abandoned and demolished and the slot trenches filled with soil. Quantities of grain have been recovered as have over 2000 flint artefacts. There was also evidence of igneous rocks being polished for axes; the local source, Tievebulliagh, is only 32km (20 miles) away. Material from further afield was also found, from the Isle of Arran and more surprisingly from the Langdale axe factory (**colour plate 4**); there are very few examples from this source

in Ireland. Most Neolithic wooden houses are rectangular and relatively small, as at the site of the earliest Neolithic house in the British Isles at Ballynagilly, Co. Tyrone. In contrast to this type of small house (and there are many other examples in Britain), is an unusual site in Scotland at Balbridie (**34, 35**).

This site was originally interpreted as an Anglo-Saxon hall site comparable to another one known as Doon Hill. The research design for its excavation was based on this assumption and until the first radiocarbon dates were received, which showed it was Neolithic, there was no need to alter the research design; in fact the excavation strategy did not change but it was critical that the *samples* for radiocarbon dating were definitely primary (i.e. not secondarily deposited). There are two ways in which this could have happened: an Anglo-Saxon house built on existing Neolithic settlement/deposits or that the trees used by the Anglo-Saxons were felled in the Neolithic and survived. However, the samples were taken from the upper fills of the trenches and post-holes; they date the filling up of the features. Ten dates ranging from 2790 ± 135 bc to 3080 ± 60 bc were taken on charred remains of cereals (the site produced over 720,000 grains of cereal); a Neolithic date cannot be much in doubt. The grain also contained evidence of bread wheat as a separate crop which is not common in the Neolithic; it was probably warm enough in the early third millennium to allow bread wheat to be grown.

To quote the authors of the interim report, 'the plant macrofossils recovered at this middle Deeside location, within sight of the Grampian massif . . . , perhaps betoken a rather more precocious stage in the agricultural colonization of the British Isles than is frequently detected in the archaeological record.' The excavators thought that Balbridie belongs more to continental European practices than other British sites, perhaps because of immigration to this east coast? The building is the widest Neolithic building in Europe and comparable to structures in the Aisne valley in France. It is the longest building in Neolithic Britain.

The Hebrides

As more and more archaeological work is done the distribution of sites of all periods becomes wider. Excavations in Scotland and especially on North Uist (in the Outer Hebrides) have revealed a number of Neolithic settlement sites (The Udal, Eilean an Tighe, and Eilean Domhnuaill). Recent excavations at Bharpa Carinish, at the southern end of North Uist, have revealed another Neolithic house (found beneath later material). There were three stone-built hearths, five shallow pits and half a dozen small post-holes. The flint assemblage suggests domestic usage, and the macroplant assemblage contained a mix of barley, wheat, crab-apple pips, and hazelnut shells. It is difficult to convey the nature of this site as the features are ephemeral, unlike the stone walls of Barnhouse, which are eye-catching when under excavation. More often the remains of Neolithic dwellings are like those at Bharpa Carinish; maybe the stone walls which surrounded the hearths have been removed, perhaps to build a cairn nearby?

This site is also like so many others in that it was discovered underneath a later more prominent monument (a long cairn). The radiocarbon dates are in the 3500–3000 bc range when calibrated. It is suggested that all hearths are contemporary (given they are 5000 years old) and they were used during a 500-year period.

In presenting this guide to Neolithic settlement I have not deliberately ignored the usually accepted centre of prehistory – Wessex; its focal point in British prehistory is not justified in terms of settlement evidence. The superb monuments which do survive (Windmill Hill, Avebury and Silbury Hill) are part of a settlement pattern in that the communities which built them must have been living nearby. Research work by the late Bob Smith has attempted to model the settlement pattern in the Avebury region. In the early Neolithic the landscape around Avebury would have been heavily wooded and although there were clearances these were not necessarily for growing crops. The woodlands were being managed for pannage (pasture for pigs), browsing for other animals and raw materials. As time went on the woodland was further opened up in the valley corridor for pastoral and arable use. There is a suggestion that new areas were needed because weed infestation, especially by bracken, had become so rampant that it was easier to open up new areas for agricultural use than it was to manage the already cleared areas. The late Neolithic was a time of dramatic social change, suggested by the large monument building which was going on in the area (Silbury Hill and Avebury). The faunal record suggests an increase in the use of pigs as they are readily renewable source of fat and protein and would have been well adapted to the local environment.

The use of the valley floor for the settlements as well as agriculture is one of the reasons finding settlement sites has been so difficult. It is this low-lying environment which has been subject to deposition and alluviation. The sites may be there, but they are difficult to find. Recently Alisdair Whittle (of Cardiff University) has been excavating large curvilinear sites in the Kennet valley, in sight of Silbury Hill; it is debatable, though, whether these sites are settlements.

Our perceptions of what life was in the 'Neolithic' and the settlements have changed dramatically in under a century. The discoveries of Skara Brae and Barnhouse and the associated monumental architecture show that socially, economically, and technologically the communities were highly skilled. In the following quotation taken from Rudyard Kipling published at the turn of the century the view of Neolithic man as a cave-dwelling savage can now be seen to be antiquated, as the century comes to a close.

Once upon a most early time was a Neolithic man. He was not a Jute, or even a Dravdian, which he might well have been, Best Beloved, but never mind why. He was a Primitive, and he lived cavily in a Cave, and he wore very few clothes, and he couldn't read and he couldn't write and he didn't want to, except when he was hungry he was quite happy. (Rudyard Kipling, *Just so Stories*, Macmillan & Co., London, 1902.)

1 *(Above) Buckland, Oxfordshire. A recently discovered causewayed camp and associated mortuary enclosure* (Crown Copyright, RCHME 4609/21).

2 *(Below) Crop marks of a late Iron Age and Romano-British site at Wolsty, Cumbria* (photograph by the author).

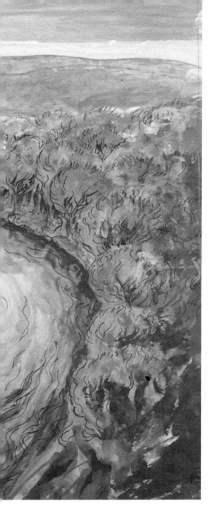

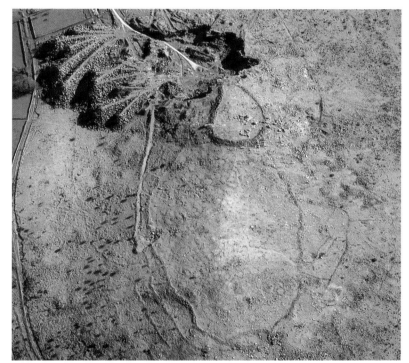

3 *(Above) Reconstruction of a Mesolithic settlement* (drawn by Timothy Taylor).

4 *(Left) Pike O'Stickle, Langdale, Cumbria. An aerial photograph of the Neolithic axe factory* (photograph by the author).

5 *(Top right) Bodmin Moor, Cornwall. Rough Tor stone-built hillfort* (Crown Copyright, RCHME SX 1480/12/333).

6 *Stowe's Pound, Cornwall. Two stone enclosures encompass Stowe's Hill, a larger one encircling most of the hill top and a smaller one which is adjacent to the more recent quarry. Inside the larger enclosure there are two Bronze Age cairns and a stone round-house. Visible on this false colour infra-red aerial photograph are a number of circular platforms (where stone has been cleared for timber houses). It is likely that this site is of a similar date to Rough Tor – late Neolithic or Bronze Age* (Crown Copyright, RCHME SX 2572/20/24).

7 (Above) Aerial photograph of the reconstruction of the Bronze Age settlement at Flag Fen, Cambridgeshire. Note the Roman road running south from the site, showing as a pale line (Crown Copyright, RCHME 4238/14).

8 (Right) Reconstruction of an Iron Age hillfort (drawn by Timothy Taylor).

9 *Aerial photograph of a low-lying Iron Age hillfort at Wardy Hill, Cambridgeshire. Note the developed entrance features* (photograph by Ben Robinson).

10 *A 'banjo' type enclosure with trackway and funnel entrance and associated curvilinear and rectilinear sites at Ashton Keynes, Wiltshire* (Crown Copyright, RCHME 4604/7).

11 (Above) Butser Hill Ancient Farm, Hampshire.
Butser Ancient Farm is an open air research laboratory
which is researching the domestic and agricultural life
of the Celtic Iron Age. It is the only place in western
Europe where ancient livestock, cereals and plants can
be seen in the context of the fences, fields and domestic
dwellings and buildings of the Iron Age. The studies at
Butser also include industrial processes such as pottery
and iron manufacture as well as charcoal burning. To
begin to understand what prehistoric life was like, a
visit to Butser is essential. See section on places to visit
(copyright: Peter Reynolds).

12 *(Far left) Reconstruction of the Iron Age settlement (c. AD 200) at Thorpe Thewles* (copyright: Cleveland County Archaeology).

13 *(Left) Airport Catering Site, Stansted, reconstruction; dated to the first century BC, it had a number of round houses arranged around a central building, which has been interpreted as a shrine. Occupation at the site was first established around 75 BC and the whole area enclosed at about 50 BC, and it is this phase which has been reconstructed* (original watercolour by F. Gardiner; copyright: Essex County Council).

14 *(Above) Glastonbury Lake Village from the air in 1966* (photograph by Jim Hancock).

15 *(Above) Reconstruction of part of the settlement at Chysauster* (drawn by Judith Dobie; copyright: English Heritage).

16 *(Below) Broch of Gurness, Orkney. Broch and later surrounding settlement* (photograph by the author).

5
Bronze Age Settlement

The past 20 years have seen a dramatic increase in our knowledge and understanding of how people lived in the Bronze Age. We know a great deal about the burial practices; antiquarians opened up thousands of barrows as a leisurely pursuit in the nineteenth and early twentieth centuries. The ubiquity of Bronze Age burials throughout Britain has allowed for the pre-dominance of the study of death for this period to continue. This is exemplified by Fox's *Life and Death in the Bronze Age*, published in 1959; in the preface the author admits the book is about Bronze Age barrow excavation!

So, was the Bronze Age any different from the Neolithic? There is a change in the landscape during the late third and early second millennia. Settlements which might be described as permanent begin to be developed and the landscape is controlled to a much greater degree. Linear boundaries can be seen as a feature of the Bronze Age throughout England, especially in Wessex, Dartmoor, and Yorkshire.

The technological change, from stone to bronze, did not happen overnight and there is good archaeological evidence for a considerable overlap. The use of bronze in Europe was normally preceded by copper artefacts, but in Britain the Copper Age is virtually non-exis-tent. At the same time there were also changes in pottery style with the arrival of beakers; finely-made, tall, and elaborately decorated pottery.

The Beaker phenomenon

Whole books have been written on the Beaker folk (2700–1700 BC) and there has been much discussion in the archaeological literature about the nature of the beakers themselves and the supposed 'folk' who used them. Were they immigrants who brought in a new bronze working technology and beakers? Or did the use of these fashionable objects spread as fashions do, by personal recommendation, trade and simple copying? Nobody admits to knowing the answer and the spread of beakers must have been a combination of movement of peoples as well as the diffusion of ideas beyond the areas where the originators moved; their distribution spreads from Algeria in the south to Norway in the north, Britain in the west and the Danube in the east. Diffusion is an unfashionable word in modern archaeology, having been popular 30 years ago, but with all trends and fashions (and in this I mean modern fashions of thinking) it is important to hang on to the better parts of past interpretations and not discard them altogether. Diffusion falls into this category and the ways in which ideas and ultimately objects move around and are copied should be part of the study of diffusion in prehistory.

The recurring theme of death and burial is nowhere better exemplified than in the Beaker period; a classic Beaker burial would have contained a 'package' of (Beaker) arrowheads, wristguards and daggers. The question of where these people lived has usually been answered from negative evidence; we cannot find the sites so they must have lived in temporary settlements which could be easily moved. However, the truth is that we do not know what the settlement system was. Even quite sophisticated tented settlements can be moved in a matter of hours; any society which had such organised burial practices is likely to have a similarly sophisticated settlement organisation. There are two reasons why finding Beaker settlements

is difficult: one is that current archaeological techniques are not sufficient to locate Beaker settlements and the other is that post-depositional factors are such that these sites may have been lost or obscured.

Belle Tout

There is, of course, always one exception and that is a cliff-top site on the south coast of England at Belle Tout (**36**). The site is situated on virgin chalk downland with cliffs rising up 84m (255ft) from the sea, only 3km (1.9 miles) west of Beachy Head. The Beaker settlement is situated in an area of high archaeological activity with round barrows and an Iron Age promontory fort nearby. The site itself com-

36 *Belle Tout, Beaker settlement where there are three sorts of house: a wide oval, built with continuous construction trench (4); a rectilinear house built with post-holes (5), and an oval one built with post-holes (6).*

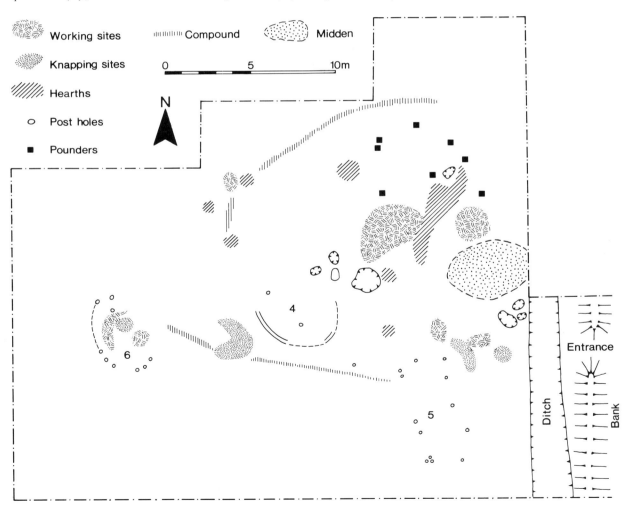

prises overlapping rectangular earthwork enclosures which have been truncated by the cliff-edge (a process which has been going for many years, at a rate of 2m (6ft) per year). The site was first discovered in 1909 and the erosion was evident then.

The excavator, Richard Bradley, suggests the site was continuously occupied (and not seasonal, as is often suggested for late Neolithic and early Bronze Age sites); this is based on the fact that the pottery is local and that there appear to be permanent structures. Cattle herding was probably important, the enclosures and other associated ditches are interpreted as stock enclosures. The large amount of flint scrapers discovered suggests that the preparation of hides was an important activity at the site.

The Beaker period is often seen as the transition from the Neolithic to the Bronze Age, although the use of metal was prevalent before the Beakers themselves arrived. The extent to which Beaker type artefacts were adopted or the 'Beaker folk' invaded is still an unresolved matter, and as with most complex questions there is no simple, or single, answer. The main point from the settlement point of view is that there is no distinctive Beaker settlement type. The second half of the third millennium and the second millennium are characterised by the dividing up of the landscape, not just into settlements but with extensive linear boundaries and field systems.

Dividing up the land

Landscapes with settlements as hamlets, clusters of houses and field systems and linear earthworks, sometimes associated with settlements are the characteristics of the Bronze Age land use. Organising the land into areas for ranching was an important activity at this time in prehistory.

It is different from the Neolithic in that extensive areas have been 'organised', even controlled, and the remains of this control have survived. As in previous chapters I shall be looking at the archaeological features and also

at the way in which we have discovered these extensive Bronze Age landscapes. The techniques of aerial and terrestrial survey developed quickly after 1945 and during the next 30 years prehistoric landscapes were discovered. They are not yet fully understood but a number, particularly in the south-west and north-east of England, have been well recorded. Between 1970 and 1980 two approaches to archaeological work were expanding. One was for preservation and the other for excavation. Preservation strategies rely on detailed surveys and more survey is being done in Britain now than ever before, as the following examples show.

Bodmin Moor, Cornwall

Bodmin Moor is one of the best preserved and accessible areas of prehistoric settlement areas in Britain. The following case-study, based on the work supplied by Nick Johnson, the County Archaeologist for Cornwall, concentrates on a small area 2km by 3km (1.25 by 1.8 miles); it develops from what was 'known' in the last century, a few settlements, cairns, stone circles, and areas of peat bogs depicted on 1st Edition Ordnance Survey (OS) maps, which were published in 1891.

The aerial photograph (**colour plate 5**) shows a stone-built hillfort, which although not on the early maps had been recorded; it may have Neolithic origins but is generally assumed to be Bronze Age. The 1976 OS revised map for the area shows this additional information, a series of settlements, linear boundaries and cairns. Much of the 'known' area was protected by legislation (as scheduled ancient monuments), but unless our surveys are comprehensive and thorough, areas and sites cannot be protected.

In 1980 an air survey plot was completed by the RCHME and material was added from this survey (**37**, **38**). This emphasises the value, and the necessity of using as many survey techniques as possible; the aerial survey involved both the taking of aerial photographs and mapping from them (**38**). This work was then followed by field

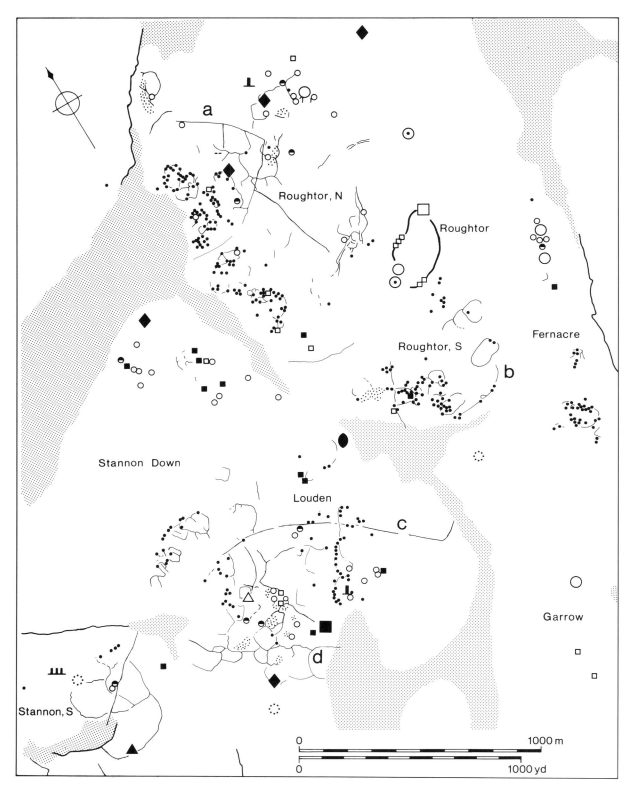

Roughtor, N

Roughtor

Fernacre

Roughtor, S

b

a

Stannon Down

Louden

c

Garrow

d

Stannon, S

0   1000 m

0   1000 yd

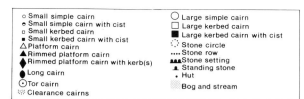

37 *Extract from the Bodmin Moor survey plan using air and ground survey techniques. The remains depicted here are probably from the Bronze Age c. 1900–1000 BC* (Crown Copyright RCHME).

survey undertaken by the Cornwall Archaeological Unit. These surveys demonstrate that it is not just a matter of adding new material but also understanding the landscape. Limited information about the stratigraphic relationship can be obtained from aerial photography, but questions about which features are earlier or later than others can only be answered by

analytical field survey (and ultimately small-scale excavation).

In analysing the landscape figure **37** shows at 'a' the curvilinear field system overlain by a major field boundary. This feature was only understood after fieldwork in 1985 and not by the previous ground surveys or the air survey.

At 'b' the settlement is overlain by a D-shaped enclosure with a linear boundary attached which runs into the bog (**37, 38**). The relationship of the D-shaped enclosure to the underlying settlement is obviously an important one. The D-shaped enclosure was interpreted through field survey to overly the settlement.

The same survey approach for 'c' showed

38 *Aerial photograph of Bodmin Moor showing settlements and fields* (Crown Copyright RCHME, SX 1480/30/286).

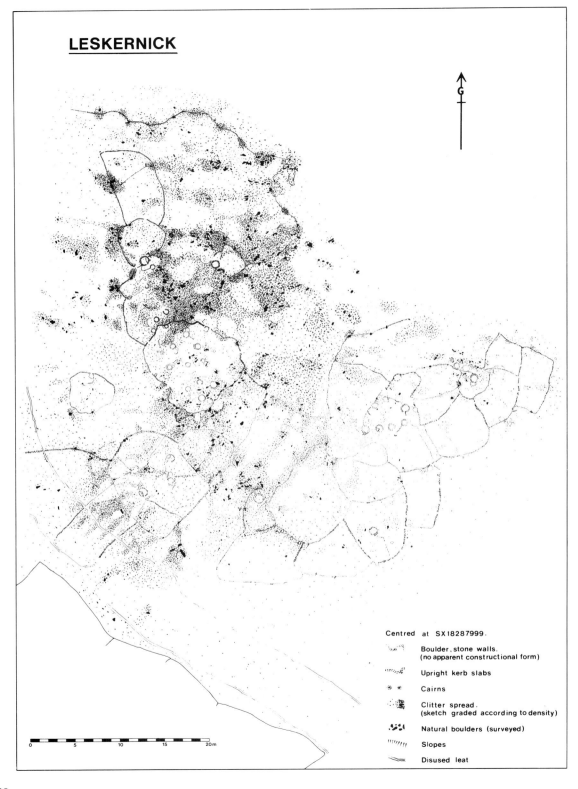

LESKERNICK

Centred at SX18287999.

Boulder, stone walls.
(no apparent constructional form)

Upright kerb slabs

Cairns

Clitter spread.
(sketch graded according to density)

Natural boulders (surveyed)

Slopes

Disused leat

0   5   10   15   20m

39 *Leskernick, Bodmin Moor, Cornwall. A stone-built Bronze Age settlement built over a long period with new circular houses and fields being added as the settlement grew* (Crown Copyright RCHME).

that the settlement and parts of field system were overlain by a major field boundary.

Similarly at 'd' the re-use of earlier field system created a major field boundary which runs into bog at the south-eastern end; more work is recommended in this area.

The purpose of going into some detail is to show the way in which archaeological surveyors think and work. The next stage is to understand and present the interpretations. Having done this analysis the chronology for the different settlements could be suggested. All fall within the Bronze Age but could be divided into time bands.

On figure **37** three different phases are represented, with three Bronze Age dates: 1900, 1500, and 1000 BC or later. Those areas which have not been closely dated are still Bronze Age but could be anywhere in the second millennium BC. Although the majority of the stone-built features are settlements, there are a few ritual monuments associated with the settlements.

Having understood in some detail one of the highest concentrations of Bronze Age archaeology there has to be a strategy for conserving the landscape. To this end the Cornwall Unit have made proposals to English Heritage. As part of a nationwide 'Monuments Protection Programme' all sites and landscapes are being re-assessed with a view to greater protection. On other parts of Bodmin Moor there are equally well-preserved sites which require detailed field survey as an aid to management and understanding, notably at Leskernick (**39**) and Stowe's Pound (**colour plate 6**).

Dartmoor

In contrast to the above part of Bodmin Moor with its settlements, there is another moorland landscape, Dartmoor, which has a network of field systems, known as reaves, and their associated settlements (**40, 41**). Although similar in date to Bodmin the contrast in land-use pattern is interesting. These reaves were originally thought to be a mixture of prehistoric (small fields) and medieval (long fields). This story is one which Andrew Fleming has described as 'A curious case of lost knowledge'. One question he raises is why, when the reaves were published in the *Proceedings of the Prehistoric Society* (not even an obscure county journal), did it take so long for their place in prehistory to be realised? The answer is partly fashion, and partly the right people in the right place with 'open minds'.

The reaves date from 1700–1600 BC and were in use for approximately 600–700 years. They were laid out in open landscape and pollen analysis has confirmed this. The word *reave* is from Old English *raew* meaning a row, whether stones, houses or walls. On Dartmoor the name reave is given to any low bank or line of stones, whatever its purpose.

The whole system of fields which criss-cross the Dartmoor landscape has had different names applied to it, aggregate or cohesive, but Fleming has coined the phrase 'coaxial' for this type of system which is laid out systematically on one major axis. Since the term was coined, coaxial systems have been found in the west of Ireland (Behy-Glenurla and on the Burren), on Bodmin Moor, in northern England in Swaledale, and at Grassington and on the South Yorkshire/Nottinghamshire border, in Lincolnshire at Goltho, at Fengate near Peterborough, in Norfolk and Suffolk and across southern England from Cornwall (West Penwith) through Dorset and Wessex to Black Patch in Sussex. This is only the tip of the iceberg and when more survey work (using aerial survey and field survey) has been done, more of these field systems will be discovered.

Figure **40** is a plan of the Dartmeet system. The houses, 'black blobs', cluster in a neighbourly way but are they all contemporary? This is one of the best examples of an articulated

40 *Dartmoor: part of the Dartmeet parallel reave system on Holne Moor showing houses and reaves. The black blobs (houses) appear to cluster into neighbourly groups (after Fleming).*

landscape; the Combestone way runs all the way across the system at right angles to the main system (in four different stretches). Ring cairns and large cairns occur within the system and just beyond the terminal reave. A triple stone row lies just beyond the terminal reave and may have helped to determine its position. The reaves have a preference for running straight up the hillside at right angles to valley or river, except where common sense prevailed and they had to follow the contour.

The settlements and individual houses were not evenly distributed but clustered; the fields furthest away from houses are relatively large and rectilinear; near the house they are much smaller, more numerous and curvilinear. It was these small irregular fields which early scholars

thought were prehistoric, the linear reaves medieval. Figure **40** shows about 40 houses on Dartmeet and about 80 fields.

Figure **40** gives a good indication of Bronze Age houses and immediate fields. There is variability in the exact detail of the houses and the reaves but they all are within fields. The Ripon Tor parallel system on Horridge Common shows well on an aerial photograph (**41**). Fleming refers to these clusters of houses as 'neighbourhood groups'; elsewhere, on Yar Tor the houses are evenly distributed in fields of large size. Some of these have their domestic enclosures around them and were perhaps part of a later additional settlement especially as Yar Tor is one of the most exposed places on Dartmoor.

Transverse reaves appear to be crucial in understanding the articulation of the settlements within the wider landscape, as they define small fields near the houses, and larger fields further away. This helps to predict where

41 *Dartmor: Ripon Tor on Horridge Common, showing the parallel reaves, which are closer together near the houses and more widely spaced away from the houses* (Crown Copyright RCHME, SX 7574/23).

settlements may have been but have been obscured or destroyed. Given this 'system' of houses and two sizes of field, what was the system of ownership? It is not easy to prove ownership on basis of land divisions but it is unlikely that the land was not divided on inheritance. Sometimes the house predates the reaves, some are contemporary and others postdate the reave system.

One major question is 'who built the system'? Was it one large organiser who owned it like an estate, or a collective action? Fleming argues for an aggregate of smaller units (neighbourhood groups) in which the community was important, if not essential to survival and not very different from many rural areas around the world today. A comparative Welsh example is the *trefgordd*, which Fleming describes as 'a working unit of co-operative dairy farming...the natural group of homesteads of relatives or neighbours acting together as a single community as regards their cattle and their ploughing'. Legally the *trefgordd* was defined as 'nine houses and one plough and one oven, and one churn and one cock and one bull and one herdsman'. The size of the

neighbourhood group can only be guessed at but it was big enough to be able to operate in an organised manner, perhaps in the region of 25. It is unlikely that there were individual farms as the domestic enclosure could not feed a family. Also there is variability of the lay-out of houses and enclosures but not all elements of a farm are exhibited and were perhaps shared amongst a community. The land was farmed by a group not individuals. There are few lanes and droveways which suggests there was no concept of ownership so perhaps there was no need for separate lanes.

There are, however, other settlements on

42 *Rider's Ring, a Bronze Age settlement on Dartmoor* (Crown Copyright RCHME, SX 6764/15).

Dartmoor which are presumed to be Bronze Age but are different (and impressive) in that they appear to be villages (**42**). Fleming sees these sites as local centres.

Dartmoor is a prehistoric landscape often viewed as marginal land; marginal in terms of agricultural production as well as marginal to the centres of population of modern Britain. It is more famous for its prison and Jamaica Inn than for its archaeology. In the Bronze Age there is evidence to suggest that Dartmoor may have been a central place, not just for settlement but also for the spiritual and ritual side of life. This returns us to the theme of not being able to separate the domestic and functional from the religious and ritual. The position of five stone circles on North Moor, which are regularly spaced, suggests they are contemporary

and might therefore be a ceremonial centre for the area. This reinforces the idea that Dartmoor was central to the Bronze age communities in the area.

It is worth mentioning a methodological point which highlights the difference between the Bodmin and Dartmoor surveys. Fleming measured in the reaves by setting up base lines by eye and offsetting, he then used an 'EDM' (an electronic distance measuring system) for accurate recording of all features. In *Dartmoor Reaves* he says: 'In landscape archaeology there is always something new to notice. Given the right level of organisation and resources, we would perhaps have plotted the Dartmeet system from air photos and field checked it in a couple of seasons. If we had done it this way, our checking would have been essentially working outwards from a piece of paper, our provisional plot; the method which we actually developed, though slower, was much more responsive to what was actually on the ground.'

43 *Shaugh Moor Enclosure 15, Dartmoor under excavation* (Crown Copyright; photo courtesy of City of Plymouth Museum and Art Gallery).

This is a fair point but there is an *interpretation stage* of working with aerial photographs, and the production of that provisional plot is enormously cost-effective especially if it is the same people who are doing the aerial photographic interpretation and the field checking. As both these examples show, there is much to be gained from using all the techniques available to us.

Before leaving Dartmoor there is another area, Shaugh Moor which has added to our understanding of the landscape and individual settlements of the Bronze Age. Traditionally it was thought that the Dartmoor area would have been visited by prehistoric people who travelled some distance to Dartmoor for use as summer pasture. Excavations at an enclosure on Dean Moor, which contained 11 stone-based buildings, was more than a summer sheepfold. There was evidence for a number of activities including spinning, pottery manufacture, corn grinding, and even cheese making. Whetstones were found in every house which suggest that bronze tools were sharpened for regular use.

More recent excavations by Geoffrey Wainwright at Shaugh Moor enclosure 15 (**43**), also provided evidence for a number of activities. This circular enclosure, had no discernible entrance (except for what was perhaps a stile) and enclosed five stone-built circular houses (**43**), each containing a saddle-quern and all but one a whetstone. The theme introduced earlier of every site being open to re-interpretation arises here; initially the site was interpreted as having been occasionally visited by small groups of people for the trade of metal and agricultural produce. This practice could have gone on for over 1000 years based on radiocarbon dates (1600–600 BC). An alternative view is that the houses were built sometime around 1700–1600 BC and the enclosure wall soon afterwards. A couple of hundred years later the buildings were refurbished and projecting stone porches added. Most of the occupation took place within the space of 400 years and the enclosure was visited only occasionally after that, but especially around 600 BC.

Before leaving the south-west there is a recently excavated site at Trethellan Farm, near Newquay, which is a good example of a lowland Bronze Age settlement with seven houses and associated 'ritual' structures. The houses were situated on a level terrace with associated fields, where there is evidence for arable cultivation. The reconstruction of House 2222 (**44**) provides a good example of the Bronze Age round house which was common throughout Britain at the time. An interesting aspect of Trethellan Farm is the continuity of use at the site; after the Bronze Age settlement had been abandoned the site was not used for nearly 900 years. As the excavator, Jacqueline Nowakowski, explains, there is good evidence for continuity of settlement from the Bronze Age to the Iron Age. At this site the continuity was not in terms of settlement; the Iron Age community used the area as a cemetery. It is possible that the remains of the houses were still visible 900 years after having been abandoned and that this gave the area a special significance, which was interpreted as in some way spiritual by the Iron Age communities.

Southern England

The theme of the round house can be continued if we move to the chalk downlands of southern England. There are two sites which summarise the state of knowledge for the Bronze Age settlement on the chalk in southern England. The first is Itford Hill, a farmstead (**45**) surrounded by fields. It was a mixed farming settlement raising crops of barley and other cereals and stock raising with sheep and oxen. Probably only one family lived here for economic and social reasons. There is some evidence of ritual activity – a chalk phallus was discovered and it perhaps represents some sort of fertility cult. The main settlement appears to have been planned and built as a complete farmstead with two sleeping huts, a weaving hut and storage hut, a cooking compound, and eight other huts serving as store rooms, barns, byres and workshops. There were perhaps 20

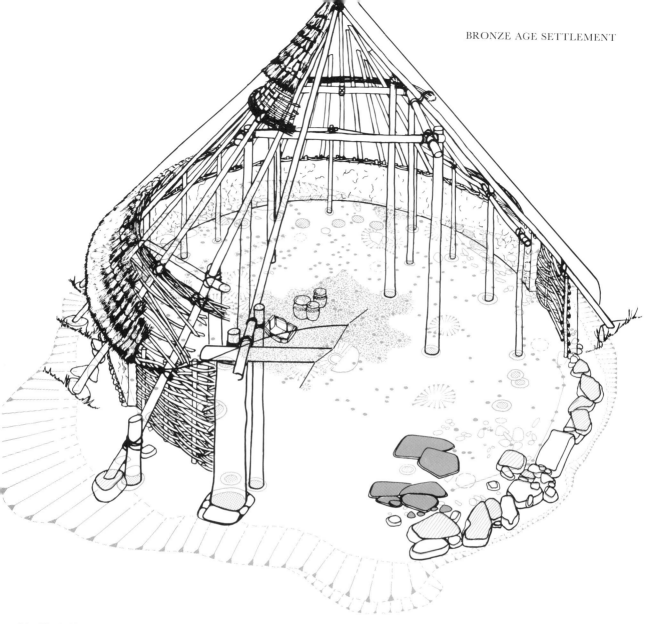

44 *Trethellan Farm, Cornwall. Reconstruction of House 2222 showing the layout of post-holes, entrance and hearth (drawn by and copyright: Rosemary Robertson).*

people living here for over 25 years. The radiocarbon dates give a range of 1000–750 BC. There is no evidence as to why the site was abandoned. In the excavation report 13 other similar sites in similar locations on the Downs are referred to, only one of these – Black Patch – has been excavated.

In 1979 Peter Drewett was able to say that the site of Itford Hill, Sussex (**45**), although excavated over 30 (now 40) years ago, is still one of our main sources for the function of Middle Bronze Age round houses. More work on similar sites was necessary to confirm and expand on the initial interpretations; one site which was excavated was Black Patch also in Sussex, only 5km (3.1 miles) east of Itford Hill. The dating of the sites through radiocarbon gives them a date of 1000 BC.

At Black Patch five certain structures were excavated and each structure was on a house

45 *Reconstruction of the Bronze Age settlement on Itford Hill, Sussex* (after P. Burke).

platform or terrace, made level from the chalk slopes. The size of the houses was always a matter for discussion and until re-interpretations in the 1970s and finally with the excavations at Black Patch (**46**) the size and construction of these houses could be suggested. They are similar in size to the later Iron Age round houses; initially the post-holes which supported the inner ring of posts was thought to be the full extent of the houses. The excavations at Black Patch revealed large areas of flint nodules which are interpreted as having been the base for the walls. The charcoal from the site was mainly from oak (with some hazel and hawthorn) and oak would have provided superb material for the post and rafters, while the other types of wood be used for making wattle walls and a framework for thatch.

Drewett's excavations also broke new ground

in recording in detail the position of all artifacts and ecofacts within the huts. Two huts of exactly similar size, shape and construction had different functions; the evidence was derived from this detailed recording and approach and was summarised diagrammatically (**46, 47, 48**). From this the social organisation of a Bronze Age community has been inferred with Hut 3 (**47**) being the chief's hut (or the Head's hut according to the excavator). The whole compound is thought to contain no more than a single conjugal family (assuming a society which had one partner each), perhaps one family with adult, unmarried siblings. The interpretation as offered in figure **47** is very much a reflection of our own society where it is assumed that food preparation is women's work and that because razors were found in Hut 3 this is a man's hut. This may in fact be

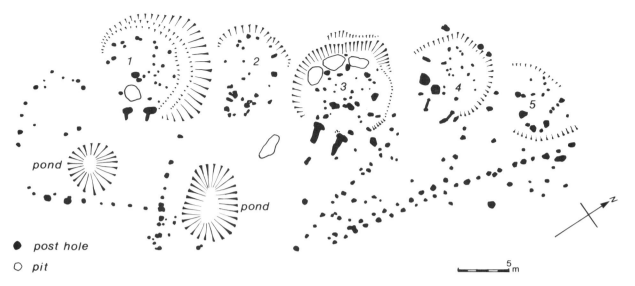

46 *Black Patch, Sussex. Plan of compound as excavated* (Drewett 1979). *See* **48** *for reconstruction.*

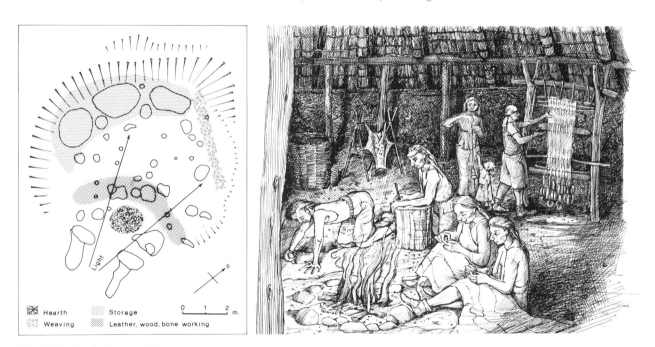

47 *Black Patch, Sussex. Hut 3 and reconstruction: layout and functional areas inside the house* (Drewett 1979).

correct but we must be wary of imposing our own values on people 3000 years ago. Did women shave in the Bronze Age? Did men prepare the food at Black Patch? Is there any reason why the Head of the group was a man (**46, 48**)?

River gravels

Having so far concentrated on upland sites, there is a wealth of information contained in the gravels of Britain, which deserves attention. As explained in the early chapters, crop marks are a common phenomenon throughout the

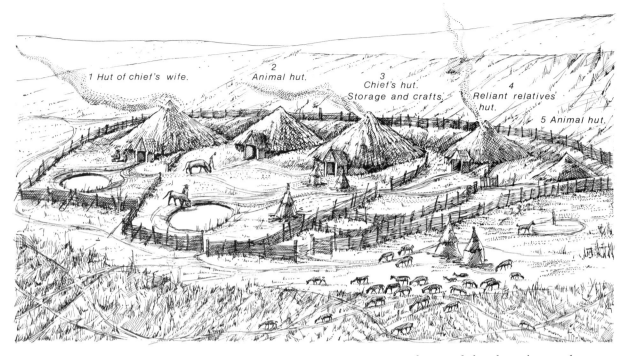

1 *Hut of chief's wife.*

2 *Animal hut.*

3 *Chief's hut.*
Storage and crafts.

4 *Reliant relatives'*
hut.

5 *Animal hut.*

48 *Black Patch, Sussex. Reconstruction of compound 4 showing houses and fields* (after Lysbeth Drewett).

British Isles, but the river gravels produce good crop marks as they are usually free draining. This biases our understanding of these areas as we are seeing only those sites which form crop marks; other sites, buried by alluvium, remain hidden until excavated. Recent work has shown that there is as much to be gained (if not more) from excavating in the river floodplains where crop marks have not formed as there is from excavating crop marks. That said, the information which we can obtain from crop-mark sites is good.

The Thames Valley is famous for its crop marks and the work of the Oxford Archaeology Unit has done much to help us understand the sites and landscape. One of the areas researched from aerial photography and excavation is the area around Reading. Here the question of the abandonment of late Bronze Age settlements in one small area of the Thames valley, the junction of Kennet and Thames, highlights the

way we can understand the changing settlement pattern in prehistory. There are eight excavated sites, *c.* 0.5–1.5km (0.3–1 mile) apart in the space of 6km, all near a high-status site, Marshall's Hill. Most of the sites are likely to have been pastoral settlements (with perhaps having some cereal production). The point of interest here is the importance of the confluence of the two rivers (Kennet and Thames), where we have good evidence for settlement (**49**) as well as an area of the densest concentrations of riverine finds of prestige metal-work in the Thames valley. Throwing your best sword, palstave or axe into the river (or whatever expanse of water was near) was an important Bronze Age ritual; linking the settlements with this ritual activity helps us understand more about the Bronze Age way of life, and the importance of natural water supply.

In the twentieth entury we tend to forget how important rivers and water supply are; our pollution goes much further than lobbing bits of bronze away. To a society dependent on a natural supply of water for drinking and daily use, as well as for longer distance communica-

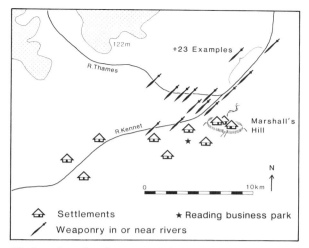

49 *Location of settlements and deposits of weaponry at the confluence of the Thames and Kennet rivers* (copyright: Oxford Archaeological Unit).

Mucking creek and ridge routeway in the nineth century BC; another nearby site formed a similar function. The linear features visible in the photograph date from the earlier Bronze Age and the later Romano-British period (there is a villa nearby). The smaller circular features are Iron Age huts and the even smaller splodges are Saxon huts which contained sunken floors. Being on the gravel terraces this area was good for settlement from the Mesolithic through to the post-Roman period; after that it would have been prime agricultural land. Therein lies the seeds of its own destruction as the plough flattened it. This enabled archaeologists to rediscover it, only for the gravel companies to obliterate the site. Excavations in the 1970s and 1980s have at least recorded the site.

tions propitiation to the gods of water can only be expected. Disposal of wealth also maintained the value of the objects. The high-status site of Marshall's Hill is also strategic, overlooking the Kennet valley and confluence of the Thames and Kennet as well as controlling route ways through the Goring Gap. It has been argued that high-status sites depended for their existence on a prestige goods economy and that the collapse of that economy may be the reason for the abandonment of settlement in this area. Other areas of the Thames valley throughout the Bronze Age may have invested in large cattle herds (which may have inhibited agricultural expansion) and there is an increasing amount of evidence for major land boundaries in the Upper Thames Valley (around Lechlade, for example) which may have been required for the control of stock.

Although the Thames Valley is a single river valley there is a huge diversity in its archaeology. In the lower part of the valley, in Essex, there is a well-known site at Mucking; this is not unique as a settlement except that it has been excavated. The prehistoric site might be described as a mini-hillfort of late Bronze Age date (**50**). The two concentric circles, which form a defended settlement, guarded the

50 *Aerial photograph of the crop marks at Mucking, Essex. The concentric double ring is a late Bronze Age 'mini-hillfort'. The rectangular outlines are of fields of Romano-British date, overlying earlier prehistoric fields* (Cambridge University Collection of Air Photographs: copyright reserved).

51 *Paddock Hill, Thwing, North Yorkshire. A defended circular Bronze Age settlement. Note also the junction of 3 double-ditched linear features, presumed to be contemporary with the defended settlement* (Cambridge University Collection of Air Photographs: copyright reserved).

Northern Britain

So far I have concentrated on southern landscapes; upland, gravel and chalk. This was deliberate as they have been under the most threat from industrial developments and urban expansion and have been intensively surveyed. There are other areas where the preservation is equally good, or better, and for which we have evidence for settlement from the Bronze Age.

The first is the chalk area of the Yorkshire Wolds of east Yorkshire which has been surveyed from the air and mapped using thousands of aerial photographs as part of the RCHME's Yorkshire Wolds project. Non-survey work in the area has focused on a site called Paddock Hill, Thwing (**51, 52**) (comparable in terms of form with the double ring at Mucking); the

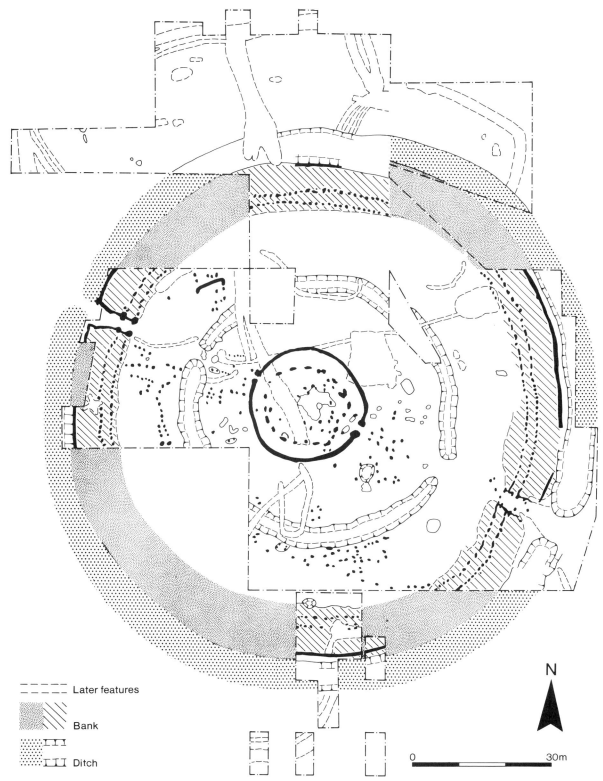

Later features

Bank

Ditch

N

0   30m

52 *The excavation plan of Paddock Hill, Thwing, a Bronze Age settlement. The outlying ditches are not Bronze Age and there is evidence of Anglo-Saxon occupation* (copyright: Yorkshire Archaeology Society and English Heritage).

site was initially thought to be a henge monument but excavation soon showed it to be a Bronze Age ringwork (defended) settlement which continued in use (intermittently) until the Anglo-Saxon period. Apart from the importance of this site, as it has been excavated, it is only one of many other sites in this area, of similar form. More significant, though, is the fact the linear features which are visible on the aerial photographs are contemporary and form part of a large network of linear banks and ditches which continue for many miles across this chalk landscape (**51**). There are now many examples of this dividing up of the landscape,

53 *Lea Green, Grassington, North Yorkshire. A late Iron Age and Romano-British enclosure with associated field systems enhanced by a light covering of snow. Other features date from later industrial activities* (Cambridge University Collection of Air Photographs: copyright reserved).

especially on the chalk downlands of England. The Yorkshire Wolds can be referred to as the Wessex of the North and it is still an important area for new archaeological discoveries.

As I have already mentioned there is more survey work being undertaken in Britain than ever before; landscapes and sites being recorded as never before. Recent work by RCHME in the Yorkshire Dales (**53**) has highlighted the

54 *Standrop Rigg, Linhope, Northumberland. A late Bronze Age settlement with field systems* (after Jobey).

need for integrated surveys as there are a number of well-preserved site and landscapes which are not yet fully understood. Fortunately Andrew Fleming is working in Swaledale and when his work has been completed we will have a better understanding of the prehistoric (and later) exploitations of the Dales.

Further north in Northumberland and southern Scotland there have been surveys and excavations by RCHME and Newcastle University. Standrop Rigg (**54**) was excavated by George Jobey and proved to a Bronze Age settlement. The dominant settlement type is the unenclosed settlement – houses, palisades but no encircling ditches, with fields beyond. Environmental evidence shows little indication of Bronze Age clearance, hence the small and unenclosed settlement pattern in this part of the north-east. The unenclosed settlement was a common form of site, often attributed to the

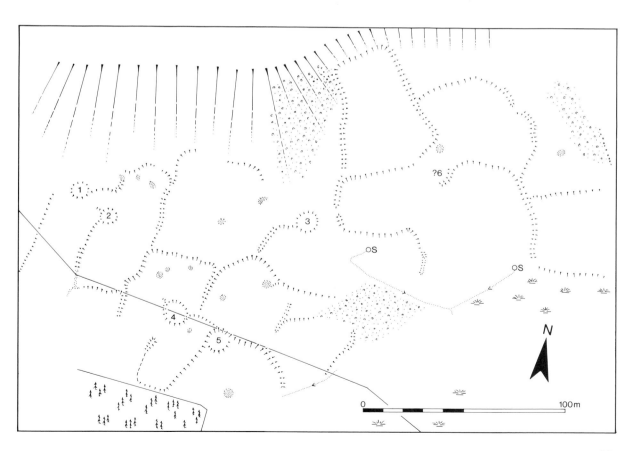

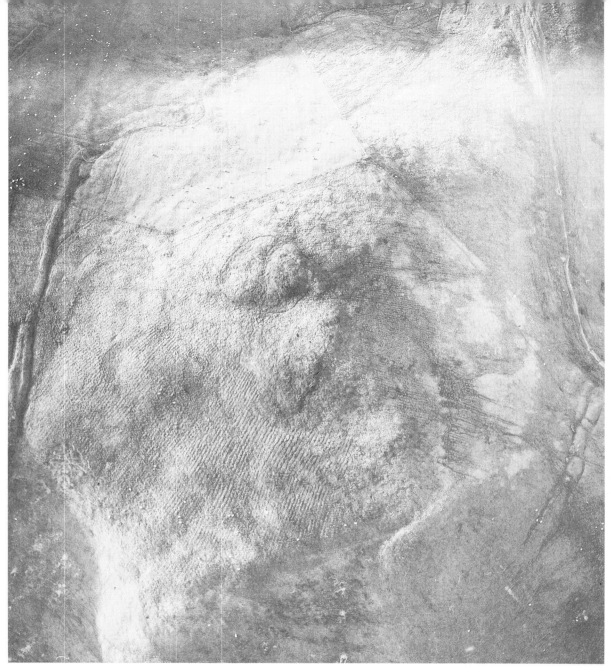

55 *Woden Law, Roxburghshire palisaded settlement and cord rig (narrow ridges formed as a result of ploughing)* (photo by Tim Gates; copyright reserved RCHME, NT 7612/2).

Bronze Age, and excavations at Black Law and Standrop Rigg have confirmed this (**54**).

A new type of agriculture has been found, a narrow system of ploughing called cord rig (**55**). This type of cultivation has been dated mainly to the Iron Age but there is much more work which needs to be done on these palisaded sites and their fields in the Borders region. Recent work by Peter Topping at Linhope Burn has helped place cord rig and associated settlement in a first millennium context.

Further north in Perthshire there have been recent surveys which have recorded the densest

86

concentrations of prehistoric settlement in Scotland in the form of hut circles (**56, 57**). A total of 845 hut circles has been recorded in heather moorland often at altitudes higher than one would expect, at 300m to 400m (950–1250ft). There has been little excavation of these features but the limited work that has been done shows that they date from the second millennium and early part of the first millennium.

Stonehenge and other sites

It had been my intention not to mention Stonehenge to any great degree in this book; for a number of reasons it is worth mentioning.

56 *Alyth Burn, Perthshire. Aerial photograph of circular houses forming prehistoric open settlements* (Crown Copyright: Royal Commission on the Ancient and Historical Monuments of Scotland).

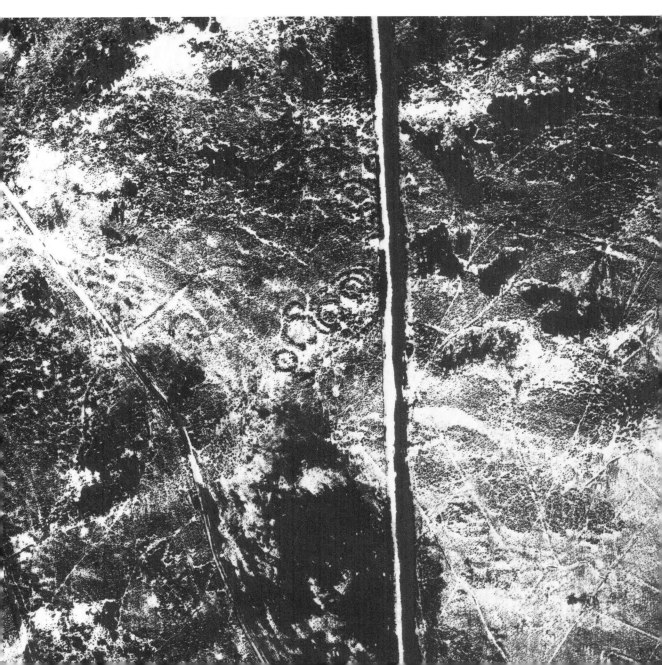

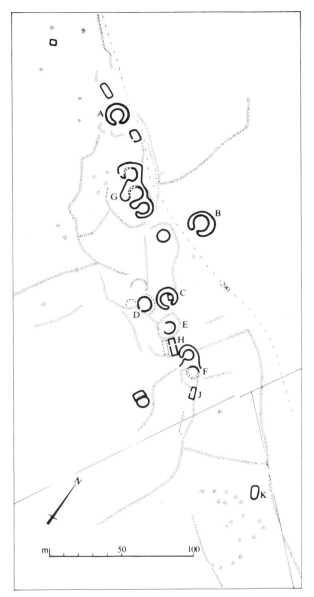

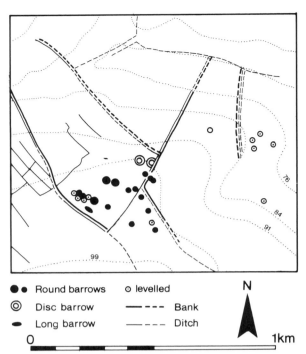

58 *Stonehenge area. Detail area around Wilsford Down showing junction of linear features settlements and barrows* (Crown Copyright RCHME).

Round barrows ● ●
Disc barrow ◎
Long barrow ●
levelled ○
Bank – – – –
Ditch – – – –
N
0   1km

57 *Plan of the prehistoric houses at Alyth Burn, Perthshire* (Crown Copyright: Royal Commission on the Ancient and Historical Monuments of Scotland).

Stonehenge is not just about the stones and the henge, it is about the landscape in which it is set. On figure **58** there are many black lines and these refer to archaeological sites of one form or another; if this particular part of what is now Salisbury Plain was so heavily *used* in the Neolithic and Bronze Age for a variety of purposes where were the people living? There are indications of settlement within a 3km (1.9 miles) radius of Stonehenge – on Rox Hill to the south and nearer, at the Winterbourne Crossroads. Both areas have field systems which may date from the Bronze Age; they are linked by a series of linear earthworks (in parts levelled), perhaps a boundary defining a territory for controlling livestock. These linear earthworks appear to meet on the top of spur on Wilsford Down; reminiscent of many other similar linear features throughout Wessex and as far north as the Wolds in east Yorkshire (**58**).

A Bronze Age occupation site has been found in Winterbourne Stoke at the Longbarrow Cross Roads (when the roundabout was being constructed). This site was probably an enclosed settlement, associated with the field system; the site as excavated contained four circular huts, three of which are illustrated here

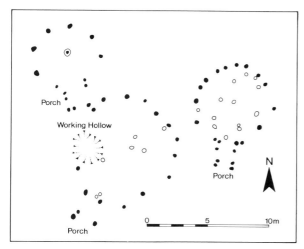

59 *Winterbourne Stoke, near Stonehenge, plans of houses from a prehistoric settlement* (after Richards).

60 *The Stonehenge landscape from the air, taken by USAF on Christmas Eve 1943* (Crown copyright RCHME).

in plan (**59**). Julian Richards warns of the difficulty of finding Bronze Age settlements in Wessex; the increased use of bronze meant that the flint tools, which are so useful in finding Neolithic sites, are not only fewer in number but also not as diagnostic as the specialised flint-knapping of the Neolithic. Therefore when poor-quality flint tools are found they are harder to date and assign the flinter scatters a Bronze Age interpretation. There are a number of possible occupation sites in the Stonehenge area according to the RCHME's Stonehenge 1979 survey. The one mentioned in Winterbourne Stoke is 2.3km (1.4 miles) from Stonehenge itself. There is another, south of the ritual enclosure, Woodhenge, 3km (1.8 miles) north-east of Stonehenge. This site was discovered through excavation by Mrs Cunnington in the 1920s but the whole extent of the site was not revealed until the drought years

of 1976; it is an egg-shaped enclosure with a trackway leading from it; the excavations indicate domestic activity from a number of pits which contained pottery and animal bones.

In the chalk landscape of Stonehenge there will have been a large amount of soil movement off the tops and slopes of the downs. Within the small dry valleys sites may have been hidden and will remain preserved until research or a pipeline is required to disturb them. When you visit Stonehenge, now or in ten years, do not concentrate solely on the Stones and the Henge; imagine yourself in a landscape which has grown up over many centuries (even by the Bronze Age the landscape had been used for thousands of years); make the time to walk around the perimeter of the landscape, as it will help your understanding of the *scale* of 'prehistoric landscapes'. The landscape may seem very localised in scale through modern eyes, but it is still broad enough to allow for a variety of activities to take place. In the Stonehenge landscape there is a 3km (1.9 mile)-long *cursus* – was it a horse racing track? There is the henge itself with an avenue leading into it which undulates with the contours of the down; and many barrows which are visible from a number of places (**60**).

Stonehenge may be the most well known of prehistoric sites but Flag Fen is rapidly becoming the best Bronze Age place to visit. This is a waterlogged-wood, wet site with good preservation of wood and artefacts. The site is currently under excavation as well as having good reconstructions open to the public. The aerial photograph (**colour plate 7**) does remind us of the three-dimensional nature of archaeology; the yellow linear feature which runs away from the reconstructed lake is a Roman road, which sits above the waterlogged wood at Flag Fen. There are few better examples of the intensity of land-use over the past 5000 years than around the fen-edge at Flag Fen.

6

Iron Age Settlement

In contrast to the preceding periods it is the settlements not burials which characterise Iron Age Britain; this is not exclusively so, but in comparison to the previous periods the numbers of hillforts and the sheer numbers of enclosures (some of which have been excavated) have given us a clear picture of population growth in the first millennium BC. This final millennium of prehistory saw the transition from the ranching farmers of the Bronze Age and the beginning of what we loosely term the Iron Age. These 800 years are famous for hillforts, farmsteads, earthworks and crop marks of enclosures with round houses, field systems, brochs, crannogs *and* so much data that few people have ventured to attempt synthesis. One who has, Professor Barry Cunliffe of Oxford University, has written the standard text and any reader who wishes to pursue this subject should read his *Iron Age Communities in Britain*. This is not to say that his interpretations are accepted uncritically and Iron Age studies, perhaps more than any part of prehistoric archaeology, are characterised by deep divisions between academics. This is in fact good for the subject, and need not concern us here. The point of mentioning it is to reinforce that there is no 'right' or 'wrong' interpretation in archaeology; only the latest fashion and the standard orthodoxy. The fashions of the 1990s will become the standard orthodoxy of the next century.

One of the main distorting factors and debates in Iron Age studies is the question of the Celts. We cannot be divorced from the times in which we live, and in western Europe today there is a huge political movement towards a closer Europe; for closer European connections the 'Celts' are important. Throughout the last decade the Celts have been promoted as a pan-European people, who, while enjoying a good fight, were talented, artistic and a thoroughly 'good thing'; the *I Celti* exhibition in Venice, television programmes and colour supplement articles keep the momentum going so that we understand the last 2000 years of history in the context of what happened in Celtic prehistory. However, beware of any interpretation which argues for a unified past personified by the Celts. It may have been supported by Brussels!

As in all archaeology, Iron Age studies are moving away from the 'famous site' (Danebury, Maiden Castle, and Glastonbury) and beginning to examine the 'landscape'. Another interesting approach is that of looking at what Iron Age people did not leave behind as well as trying to understand settlements from what was left behind. As we have seen in the Mesolithic, the information in middens provides us with detailed information on human behaviour. If we imagine that we suddenly deserted, or even deliberately cleared out our current houses and settlements, what would we leave for the archaeologists of the future? There would be an abundance of information about the house and its construction but little about the people

61 *The location and names of Iron Age tribes, according to Julius Caesar.*

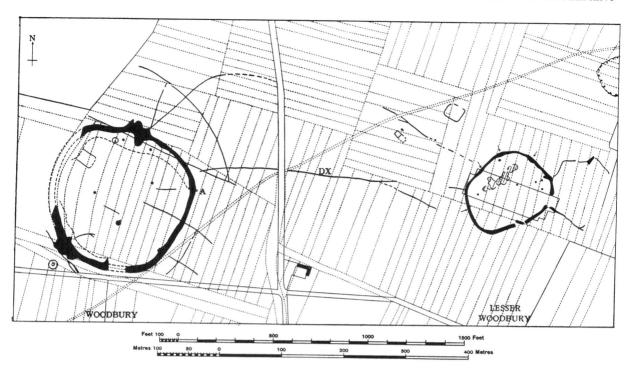

62 *Plan of the Iron Age enclosures at Woodbury and Little Woodbury in relation to the cultivation system on estate maps of c. 1600 and 1703* (broken black).

who lived there, what they ate and how they behaved. As we will see later, it is the lack of 'rubbish' on many sites which has been overlooked. While we often say how much information we have for the Iron Age, this is only true in comparison with the Neolithic and Bronze Ages.

A recent article begins with the phrase 'the Iron Age is boring'. It is, however, posed more as a question than a statement; in reality, the Iron Age is perhaps one of the most interesting times to study. There is such a wealth of information relating to the sites in the Iron Age which reveal in some detail the way of life. By the time of the arrival of the Romans, coinage and writing have been introduced and there can be seen to be some organisation among the tribes, which we can name, thanks to Caesar (**61**).

Iron Age settlement is a huge subject which cannot be easily condensed, so only a flavour

can be presented here, taking a few examples from a variety of locations. Iron Age studies reflect the history of archaeology in general; initially high-status sites were subject to campaigns of excavation by high-status archaeologists (Sir Mortimer Wheeler excavating at Maiden Castle and Professor Barry Cunliffe at Danebury). This attitude reflects the single-site approach which has to be the beginning of any archaeological study. The most visible sites (large earthworks on hill tops), like the round barrows of the Bronze Age, were the focus of attention until the study of landscapes became possible with aerial photography and more extensive fieldwork programmes.

It is instructive to look at the excavations of farmsteads. The first one was in 1938 under very unusual circumstances at Little Woodbury (**62, 63**) by Gerhard Bersu (a German 'refugee' who was eventually 'interned' on the Isle of Man for the duration of the Second World War); the next excavation was not until 1960 with the excavation at Pimperne, Dorset (and Longridge Deverill Cow Down). Woodbury

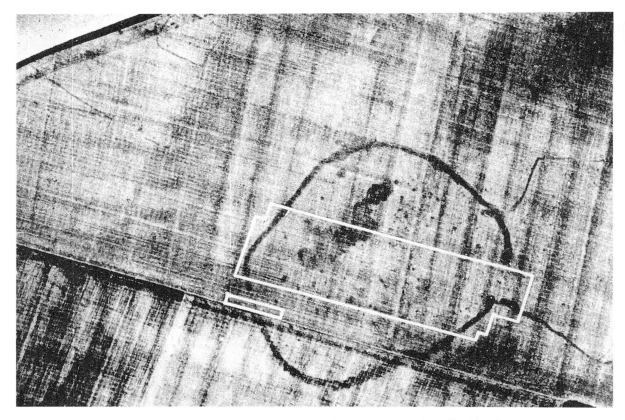

63 *Little Woodbury as photographed by OGS Crawford, with the excavation trench outlined in white* (Crown Copyright RCHME, SU 1427/13/IA).

was published in *Proceedings of the Prehistoric Society* for 1940 and Pimperne (same internal area as Danebury hillfort) was not published until 1993 (**64**). Both excavations had a profound effect on the way in which the Iron Age was under understood for two generations. Woodbury became the name of a 'type of culture' and the Pimperne house was the basis for a reconstructed round house at Butser Hill. The Butser experiment has been one of the most sustained archaeological scientific studies undertaken this century in this country and has maintained a high public profile throughout. A visit to Butser is essential for understanding prehistoric settlement (**colour plate 11**).

Hillforts

A few hill tops were defended in the Neolithic – Carn Brea and Crickley Hill, Windmill Hill,

Hambledon Hill and Maiden Castle. For 2000 years there was little sign of fortification, until end of the second millennium BC and a number of hill tops were defended or protected by ramparts and ditches – sometimes palisades; e.g. Norton Fitzwarren in Somerset, Rams Hill (Berkshire) and later at the Briedden, Powys. In eastern England from Yorkshire to Kent a number of ring forts have been excavated, for example Paddock Hill, Thwing (**52**). Springfield Lyons (Essex) and Mucking (Essex) show how they contained a few circular houses and, judging from the high-status objects, were perhaps fortified homesteads.

The construction of Iron Age hillforts indicates a change in the organisation of society. Early interpretations favoured an invasion of new people which brought iron with them. But was this what happened? Trade and contacts

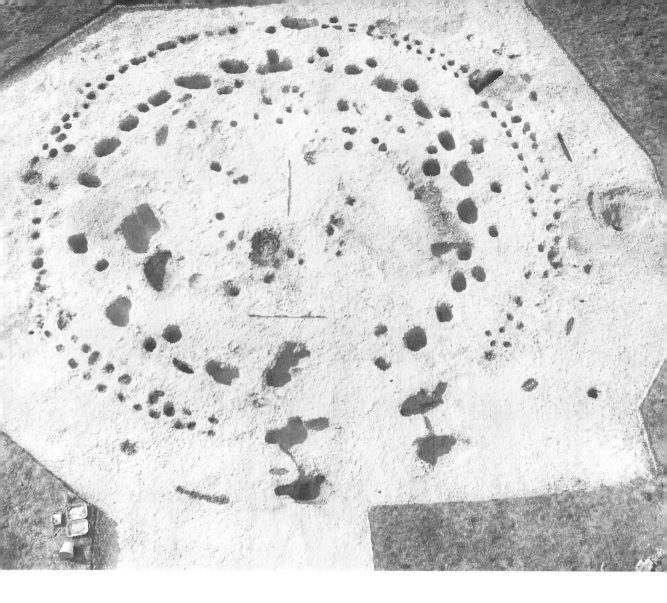

64 *The excavation of the round house at Pimperne, Dorset* (copyright: I.M. Blake and D.W. Harding).

were growing but these early explanations of how society changed were too simplistic.

Excavators at Maiden Castle (**7, 65**) reflect the changes in twentieth-century theories. Sir Mortimer Wheeler, who excavated there in the 1930s, was of the invasion theory school. In the 1980s English Heritage arranged a large-scale re-evaluation at Maiden Castle and the excavator, Niall Sharples, espouses an altogether less simplistic view. He argues that the invasion hypothesis assumes a relatively static model for all societies, and this has been shown to be not the case. Work over the last 30 years, by anthropologists and sociologists, has shown that all societies are dynamic and are always changing. Often this change is imperceptible in the archaeological record, but the major changes are recoverable.

Sharples' theory is that the desire for change amongst the Bronze Age people, in which trade networks were established, and in which bronze was fundamental, could also be achieved through the introduction of iron; especially if

65 *Maiden Castle, Dorset. One of the most impressive Iron Age hillforts in England* (Crown Copyright RCHME, SY 6688/113).

ancient (presumed prehistoric, pre-Roman) enclosure on a hill top or similar location. The ditches and ramparts can be large and numerous earthworks as at Maiden Castle (**65**), or slighter single stoneworks as at Carrock Fell in Cumbria. By using the term hillfort we are assuming a defended place, probably a settlement. A common theme of early twentieth-century interpretations saw hillforts as refuges in times of crisis; a clarion call would be sounded and all the farmers and families would down tools and rush up to the hill top in advance of an attack. This was the image I had instilled into me from an early age (or I dreamt it up myself!). This was a favourite interpretation for Carrock Fell as the Romans built at least three military camps within 7km (4.4 miles) of the hillfort. No doubt some of the hillforts in the country did fulfil this role but there are many other possible interpretations.

Hillforts as a 'class' of site did develop through time; not just a proliferation of sites but also a development in size, shape, number of ramparts and ditches, entrance design and function. In this way they are a reflection of the society of the time.

There are over 1350 hillforts in England excluding those found in Cumbria, Northumberland, Durham, Cleveland, the Isle of Man and Scotland. These latter areas have superb hillforts, even if they are so few in number (**66, 67**). The main syntheses of hillforts have concentrated on those in England and Wales. They have been classified into two main categories of forts – 'promontory fort' and 'contour fort', with two sub-divisions for each category of 'hill-slope fort' and 'plateau fort'. These are self-explanatory terms but they do beg the question of the overall label 'hillfort'. Clearly there is a marked difference between a defended enclosure on a 'hill slope' and a 'hill top'; although there may be better terms than 'hillfort', it is commonly accepted that to attempt to change it would be difficult. The problem here is with the overall label and for convenience the term hillfort has to be used, as

there was a growing population, not all of whom could control the trade or production of bronze. New sources and new networks could be built up to the exclusion of the old 'bronze' system. Technological developments are often the catalyst for change and, although we might never fully understand the mechanics of the change from bronze to iron, the manifestation (new settlements in prominent places) is easy to record. It is also apparent that the population increased in certain areas; it is not just that we find it difficult to locate Bronze Age settlements in comparison to the Iron Age ones. There are many more Iron Age settlements and therefore we must conclude there was a much larger population which had a well-organised structure.

The term 'hillfort' as a class of monument is like any grouping – an oversimplification and a handy label. The term hillfort refers to any

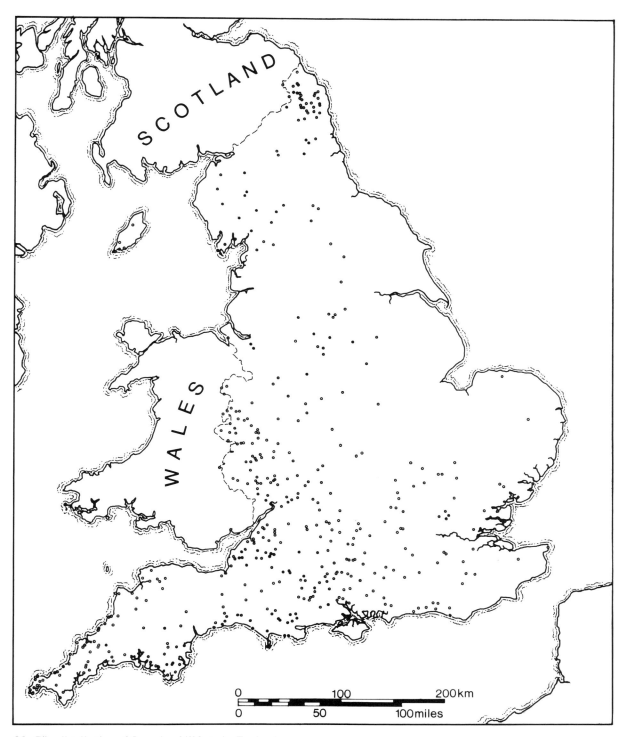

66 *The distribution of Iron Age hillforts in England*
(produced from information provided by RCHME).

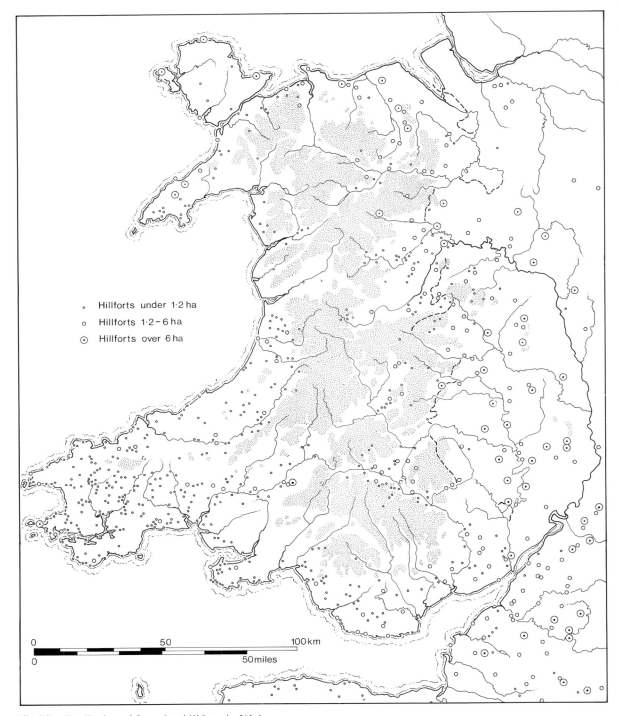

67 *The distribution of Iron Age hillforts in Wales*
(produced from information provided by C. Musson).

68 *Hod Hill, Dorset. The Iron Age hillfort and Roman fort from the air* (Crown Copyright RCHME, ST 2510/45/205).

long as it is understood that some sites in this category are not forts and are not on hills!

Another method of dividing up these sites is by size and location and in James Dyer's Shire Archaeology book on hillforts this is what he has done. There are hillforts which date from the eighth to sixth century BC which he describes as *hill-top enclosures*, 6–20ha (15–50 acres) in extent, with four-post buildings and circular huts inside; they often have weak defences, a good example is Norbury camp in Gloucestershire. Another category is the *fortified enclosures*: strongly defended with timber and stone, sometimes with two ditches (bivallate) and sited on the end of prominent spurs and ridges, and 2–4ha (5–10 acres) in size. Their strategic location is important and they are usually later than the hilltop enclosures. Good examples would be Lidbury camp in Wiltshire, or Caer Caradoc, near Chapel Lawn in Shropshire.

The main period of hillfort construction was in the sixth to fourth centuries BC with *contour* and *plateau forts*, approximately 5ha (12 acres) in extent, with timber or stone-faced ramparts and a 'V'-shaped ditch. The general interpretation is that local chieftains were in conflict

with each other and defended centres were necessary. They were also a symbol of power and some of these hillforts in some areas became the *developed hillforts*; well defended, with multiple ramparts – Maiden Castle, Hod Hill (**68**) and Danebury. Maiden Castle and Hod Hill were attacked by Vespasian in AD 45 in his attacks on over 20 places; the extent to which hillforts were built in response to the Roman invasion is a matter for debate but it is interesting to note that at Hod Hill one corner of the hillfort has been converted into a Roman fort (**colour plate 8** shows a reconstruction of the more developed type of hillfort).

69 *Hillforts in Wessex with theoretical territories based on Thiessen polygons* (after Cunliffe).

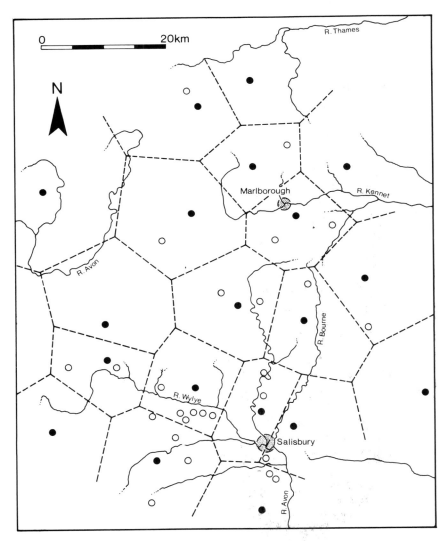

It has been suggested that certain hillforts cannot have been defended (Scratchbury in Wiltshire) because the whole of the interior is visible from below. (This gives any would-be attacker the distinct advantage of being able to see any defensive deployments.) So if defence was not the primary purpose what was the function of the site? One theory is that from a highly visible monument certain activities would take place which spectators (outside) could see, but not intrude on or intervene. The exact location of Scratchbury, for example, suggests a procession of some sort (a not uncommon practice earlier in prehistory given the 'avenues' at Avebury, Stonehenge and in the Millfield basin). Scratchbury has a number of barrows adjacent to it with a circular enclosure beyond the barrows along the ridge top. Perhaps these enclosures were ceremonial centres, at least for part of their existence.

Hillforts have usually been assumed to represent a society based on tribal chiefs (**69**). This has been questioned recently and the excavations in the Fens at Wardy Hill, Coveney (**colour plate 9**) have been used to add to the debate. The paucity of Iron Age occupation in the fens has been commented on since the 1920s; the lack of an Iron Age population was thought to be either risk of infection from malaria (given the wet conditions) or the accelerated population growth in the neighbouring fertile uplands. The environment (the topography) has to be understood at a local scale, especially in the fens; every minor hillock and ancient water course (**70**) would have its significance. The known Iron Age sites south of the Fens are all univallate and circular (**71**), whilst those in the fen are much complex. Wardy Hill ringwork (**colour plate 9**), on a spur of Ampthill clay on the north side of the Isle of Ely, seems to be of the developed kind of hillfort and is situated at 6.0m (20ft) above OD. This siting has been described as 'strategic', as 6.0m (20ft) represented the difference between dry land and being submerged!

The form of the site is such that had it

been an earthwork on a similarly strategic hill elsewhere it would have been an important hillfort. The results of the excavations at Wardy Hill have shown that it is probably a high-status site but the cause of its abandonment probably led to the occupants taking their wealth with them. As the excavator Chris Evans states in an interim report: 'It is essential we consider what would have been involved in the abandonment of a site when faced with rising water levels. This is not a matter of Atlantis like incidence...; it would entail a period of cognitive assessment leading to a decision to pack-up one's worldly goods and move. At Wardy Hill we did not recover swords, shields, cart fittings, nor other readily accepted markers of Iron Age social hierarchy. Yet, given the abandonment scenario as outlined above, one would not expect to.' This theme of what was left behind and site-formation processes will be picked up later.

As the hillfort developed it is easier to see its function as a defended place, like a walled town (foreshadowing the later *oppida*, see below), operating as a centralised distribution centre, military barracks or protected farmstead. It played an important part in Iron Age society and continues to do so today as a refuge for people to escape their twentieth-century settlements.

Questions on how long did it take to build a hillfort are difficult to answer as the local conditions would affect this greatly. An average guess is 200 men four months, at a time of stress, but what caused this stress? Was it as a result of immigration or population expansion? Archaeologists cannot agree on this but there is a huge amount of evidence for the expansion of farming which does indicate an increase in population, especially in the last centuries before the Roman invasion.

Hillforts about 6ha (15 acres) in size were constructed in Dorset in the early Iron Age. They had self-sufficient communities with sizable grain storage facilities; control of land rather than status (status was defined by trade

70 *The landscape of the Fens from the air. The ancient river system and creeks (called roddons) can be seen as lighter marks with the recent drainage pattern and rectilinear modern fields superimposed on this landscape between Peterborough and Chatteris* (Cambridge University Collection of Air Photographs: copyright reserved).

for bronze shields and swords in the Bronze Age) was the way forward in the Iron Age new economy. Defended sites with rich agricultural land were the power base for local chiefs. Maiden Castle developed more than others

because it was well placed to exploit these local resources. Control of people in the Iron Age was through land, produce and storage. This is a good model for the capitalist world in which we live, and it therefore has to be questioned, but the evidence does point to a strong ruling class.

Maiden Castle developed from 450 BC; the area enclosed by the hillfort increased from 6.5ha (16 acres) to 19ha (47 acres), taking in the area on the hill-top to the west of the existing hillfort. The only comparable site is

Hambledon (**29**), which began in the Neolithic (see causewayed camps above) but in the Iron Age increased to 8.1ha (20 acres) and then again to 12.5ha (30 acres). Other hillforts expanded in size in Dorset but they were further apart than the smaller ones; surely a clear suggestion of territorial and tribal control. The smaller hillforts may have been abandoned at this time and their communities incorporated into the lowland external settlements. Sharples

71 *Belsar's Hill, ringwork in the lowlands of Cambridgeshire. Note the way in which the medieval field system has used the ramparts of the hillfort* (photograph by Chris Cox).

suggests that the occupants of the early Iron Age site at Poundbury moved to Maiden Castle and forced the occupants of Chalbury hillfort to abandon their defence in favour of undefended lowland settlements. If this was as result of warfare, there is little evidence for an armed conflict.

Hambledon Hill (**29**) is the only other hillfort to achieve anything like the status which Maiden Castle achieved. It appears that Hambledon Hill was abandoned during the middle Iron Age and moved to Hod Hill (**72**). Hod Hill had originally been occupied in the Bronze Age but was abandoned when Hambledon Hill was occupied. Only when expansion was

HOD HILL, STOURPAINE

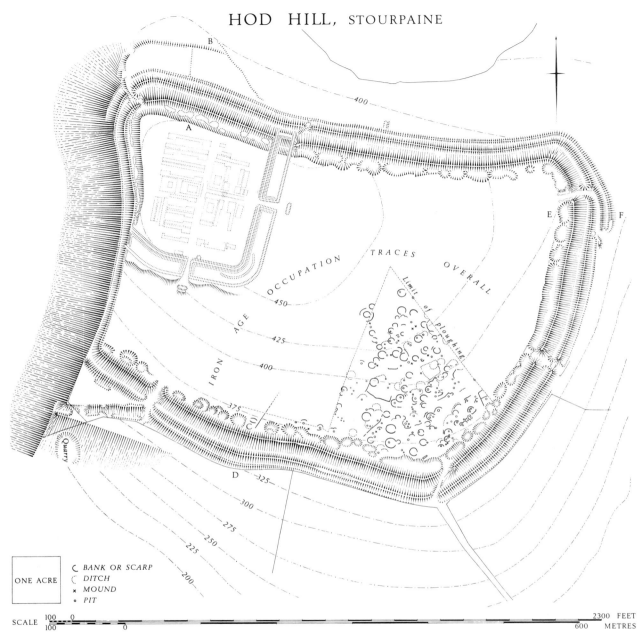

72 *Hod Hill, Dorset. An Iron Age hillfort and Roman fort. Note the hut circles in the south-east quadrant which have not been ploughed; see also the aerial photograph, page 99* (Crown Copyright RCHME).

necessary at Hambledon Hill was Hod Hill re-occupied. It was in use in AD 45, when all Durotrigian forts (the Durotriges were the local tribe) were attacked by Vespasian.

Apart from the impressive earthwork defences of banks and ditches those hillforts which have been partially excavated reveal some interesting internal details. A very common feature are 'four-posters', a square or rectangular arrangement of four post-holes. These are regular features inside hillforts in

England and Wales, but are they houses, are they storage, or exposure platforms for the dead? Are they watch towers or granaries? The latter interpretation is the most likely if the

point about control of land and food is correct.

The distribution of hillforts in Wales has been published by Chris Musson (**67**) in his report of his excavations at the Breiddin hillfort. Apart from the density of hillforts it is interesting to see the size distinctions, with smaller forts in the south and west and a series of large and larger forts in the Marches, between Wales and England. One particularly impressive site is Tre'r Ceiri, on the Lleyn peninsula (**73**). This is a large defensive village within double stone

73 *Tre'r Ceiri hillfort on Lleyn peninsula, Wales. Its commanding position overlooking fertile land and the coast led to a long occupation of the hilltop from the prehistoric through to the late Roman period* (Cambridge University Collection of Air Photographs: copyright reserved).

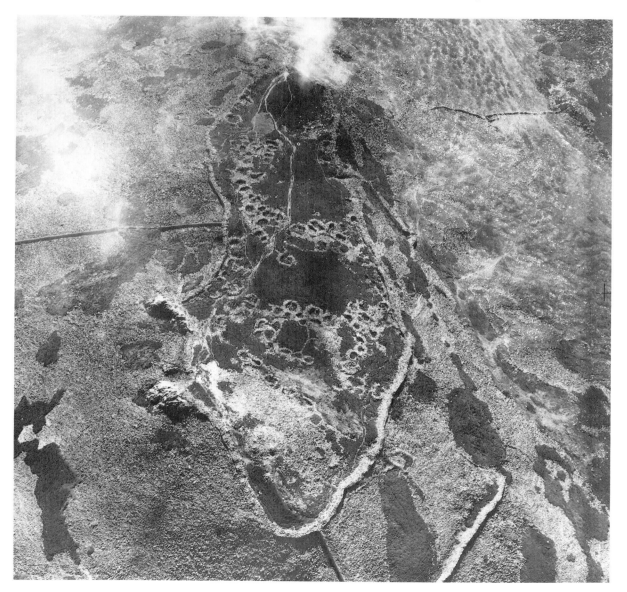

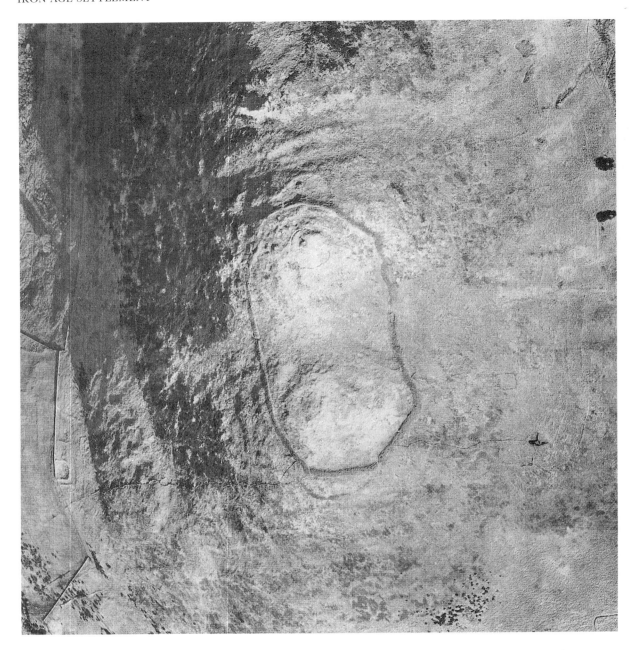

74 *Yeavering Bell, Northumberland, topped by a Bronze Age cairn and stone-built hillfort* (Crown Copyright RCHME, NT 9229/10/53).

ramparts with numerous stone-built hut circles inside, and is reckoned to date from the last few centuries before the Roman conquest and continuing into the first millennium AD.

Before leaving hillforts there are the stone-built hillforts of northern England and Scotland. Yeavering, on the summit of Yeavering Bell in Northumberland (**74**), surrounds the top of a steep hill and encloses an earlier Bronze Age cairn, clearly visible on the aerial photograph. On the slopes of the hill there are a number of other features, enclosures and fields which are presumed to be contemporary with the hillfort. The date of the hillfort is uncertain but it is presumed to be Iron Age.

Another striking example of a northern hillfort is on the summit of Ingleborough in the Yorkshire Dales near Ingleton (**75; back cover**). This magnificent setting for a hillfort incorporates a stone rampart which encircles most of the summit and a number of stone rings which are presumed to be the stone foundations for houses.

This site is worth visiting but the only threat to it is from those who visit and add stones to the large (modern) cairn; the stones are often taken from sensitive archaeological structures – so if you do visit 'take only photographs, leave only footprints and kill only time' (to quote from the sign at another hillfort, Crickley Hill in Gloucestershire).

The Iron Age round house

Perhaps the most common feature of the Iron Age is the round house (**77; colour plate 11**). Examples of these are found on virtually every Iron Age site be it a hillfort or a small farmstead. The round house was the everyday living quarter of the family in the Iron Age; its size was dependent on the status of the occupant but it was where the cooking, eating, socialising and sleeping took place on Iron Age sites. If you visit Butser Ancient Farm in Hampshire (**colour plate 11**) you will see a reconstruction of a large Iron Age house (from Longridge Deverill Cow Down). The floor area of this house is over 205 sq. m (2000 sq. ft) and it is immediately apparent that this size of house would have been an important focus on any site. There are also two smaller houses reconstructed (based on evidence from Glastonbury) and these were probably for keeping stock in (if the high phosphate levels from another round house, at Moel-y-Gaer, really does represent the remains of manure). The contrast in size between these types of round house (with apparently no intermediate size) is not only noticeable but also not fully understood.

The round house structure is a cone sup-ported by a cylinder, with the outer wall a ring of posts with wattle and daub (clay) in between the posts. Often there was an inner ring of posts for supporting the roof. It has been noted that the doorway of the large round houses is unusually large, more like a barn door than a house door; it is possible that waggons were used to bring in material which could have been stored in the area in the 'cone' of the roof. The roof would have been at a 45° angle, making the apex of the roof 8m (25ft) above the ground. The roof would have been made from rafters which would have been thatched. The structural techniques and details of roofing and thatching are well presented at both the Butser Ancient Farm, Chalton, Hampshire for the Iron Age and at Flag Fen, near Peterborough for the Bronze Age.

In social terms we know very little about the round house. One theory is that the space within the house could have been divided into two; the middle (central) area which was the 'public' space and the outer ring (between the inner ring and the outer wall) being the 'private' space. This theory is influenced by the structuralist philosophies of Levi-Strauss in which binary oppositions of public and private, or male and female, cooked and raw, are used as explanatory tools, but they may not have operated in the Iron Age (or any 'Age' for that matter). It is unfortunate that with so many anthropological studies about houses and communities we do not have better developed theories about the Iron Age round houses. The public and private dichotomy is a starting point but with properly oriented research excavations it may be possible to learn more about the way in which all the aspects of Iron Age societies functioned. We are not really clear about the organisation on a daily or annual basis.

Recent research has shown that the entrances of Iron Age round houses have a tendency (**76**) to be oriented towards midsummer sunrise and the autumn equinox (north-east through east to south-east). This has led to the suggestion of splitting the use of space within the house along

INGLEBOROUGH   CRAVEN   N. YORKS.

SD 77 SW 1

Crown copyright

RCHME

MCBB CMSS NKB

Aug. 88

░░░░ Turf-covered stone bank

╲╲ Bare stone bank

▣ ⌐ Modern structure

┈┈ Extent of major tourist erosion – August 1988

75 *Plan of the hillfort at Ingleborough, North Yorkshire. The stone ramparts and over 20 hut circles are very fragile; note the area of erosion (dashed line) caused by visitors removing stones from the hut circles and adding them to the 'walkers' cairn'* (Crown Copyright RCHME).

an east-west axis. The evidence from Longridge Deverill Cow Down round house (which was burnt down) shows that the left (south side) of the house contained large quantities of occupational debris, whereas the right (north side) of the house was devoid of any occupational debris. Mike Parker Pearson and Colin Richards also argue that this east-west dichotomy is evident in most settlement enclosures and if the enclosures have a north-south divide they are not settlements. This suggestion needs further investigation and detailed analysis but it provides a hypothesis which can be tested by a number of projects which are currently taking place in England, which involve mapping all archaeological sites from the air. The orientation of the entrance of each enclosure is being recorded.

The question of the roles of men, women and children in prehistoric society is often asked. Did they have particular roles as anthropological

76 *Orientation of entrances of Iron Age houses* (after Oswald).

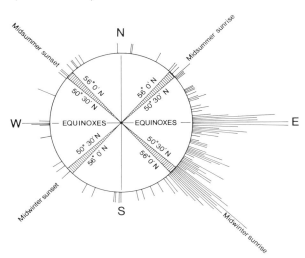

studies suggest they should do? Some would argue archaeological techniques are not capable of throwing more light on these questions. This may be so but it still should not deter us from attempting to find out. As mentioned above, recent work by J.D. Hill on site formation processes and the Iron Age highlights a significant weakness in the information we obtain from Iron Age sites; the lack of domestic rubbish is surprising but seems to be true.

For example in the early Iron Age phase at Winnal Down one pit was filled every 7–10 years (based on the excavated data); only one rim sherd would have been lost every 9–12 months, given a 200-year occupation! If an Iron Age pot weighed 1kg (2lb) and only 25.8kg (56lb) were found then this is not a representative sample of Iron Age pottery; where has it gone? At Danebury a loom weight or comb would have been lost every two years given the number recovered from the excavations; similarly there are only 100 identifiable bone fragments a year, from a population estimated to be between 250 and 500 people. So, although it might be stretching a point to say the sites are 'clean' the amount of rubbish which 200 people leave per year was obviously being removed from the site and our interpretations will have to reflect these biases.

Future studies will have to involve the density of settlement within the hillfort or farmstead. Suggestions have been made of 15 persons per acre inside a hillfort, others say this is too high and others too low. Another proposal is 25 persons per acre. If we take the lowest figure then for Maiden Castle at its height there would have been over 700 people living there. It is difficult to know how correct this is especially given the fact that a hillfort such as Maiden Castle was more than just a place to live.

So often in archaeology we present information about sites or landscapes which seem complete and whole; we forget that we are dealing with human behaviour and the results of success and failures. Ladle Hill in Hampshire is a good example of what has been described

77 *Reconstruction of life in a round house at Carn Euny, Cornwall.* (J. Dobie; copyright: English Heritage)

as an 'unfinished hillfort'; the banks (**78, 79**) appear to be no more than the dumped upcast from the ditches. The causes for such a circumstance can only be guessed at, but the site has other interesting features. The linear earthworks and rectangular enclosures which can be seen on the aerial photograph (**79**) are evidence of organising a landscape for pasture and cattle herding. The linear earthworks may be earlier than the hillfort.

Danebury (**80, 81**) is one of the most famous of all Iron Age hillforts but it is its landscape on which I want to dwell. The hillfort was excavated over 20 seasons, finishing in 1988 with over half the defended area being excavated.

But what about the 'landscape context' in which it was set? The work of Rog Palmer analysing and interpreting aerial photographs of the surrounding landscape formed the basis for the Danebury Environs Projects (under the direction of Professor Cunliffe). This seven-year project (1989–95) is still going on but aims to examine the evolution of the landscape in the first millennium BC and first millennium AD. The results are so far of an interim nature, and Professor Cunliffe has written: 'It has been a salutary warning to those of us who like to make generalising statements about Iron Age society that each of the field work programmes...has demanded significant readjust-

78 *An early aerial photograph of Ladle Hill, Hampshire, an Iron Age hillfort* (Crown Copyright RCHME, SU 4756/11).

110

◄ **79** *Ladle Hill showing the associated linear features (middle right especially) and Bronze Age barrows* (Crown Copyright RCHME, SU4576/66).

80 *Danebury, Hampshire, from the air during the excavations in 1975* (Crown Copyright RCHME).

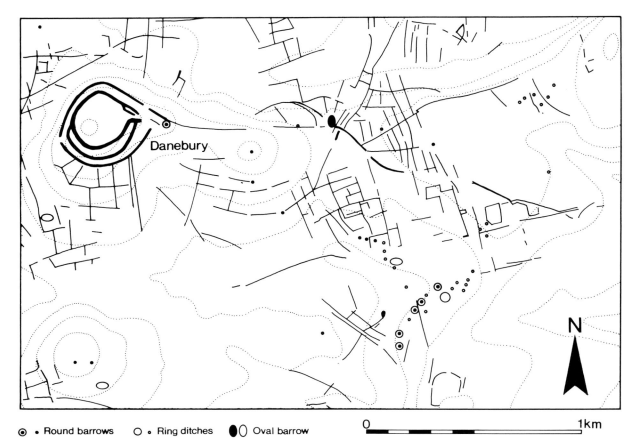

⊙ • Round barrows   O • Ring ditches   ●O Oval barrow

0 _____ 1km

81 *Danebury area: an extract from a survey of aerial photographs showing the hillforts, field systems and barrows* (Crown Copyright RCHME).

ments to comfortable preconceptions – how disorienting new data can be!'

The work is setting the hillforts of Danebury, Woolbury and Bury Hill in their landscape contexts. The landscape around Danebury is a complex pattern of linear boundaries and field systems (**81, 82**), which have been revealed by aerial photography and presented clearly by Rog Palmer in an RCHME survey.

Farmsteads

The Iron Age is also characterised by a huge number of 'farmsteads'; these manifest themselves in a number of ways but they are most often seen as curvilinear and rectangular crop marks, as already shown for Woodbury (**62,**

63). There is a number of excellently preserved stone-built sites, and Carn Euny (**77**) is a very good example and well worth visiting, not least to crawl down the fogou (a subterranean chamber). The stone houses which are visible today are the later replacements of earlier wooden ones.

The distribution of Iron Age farmsteads has never been mapped but they are found throughout Britain in some form or other. A striking example of one which has been excavated is Thorpe Thewles in Cleveland. It was the highest open excavation of an Iron Age defended site in North England with two distinct phases. The site started as a defended enclosure in 200 BC (**colour plate 12**) and then became an open settlement with internal partitions by AD 50. The economic base for the site was mixed farming with cattle being the predominant source of food. Sheep were also an important secondary resource for food and wool with pigs also being reared.

The reconstruction of Thorpe Thewles (**colour plate 12**) and of another similar site, in Essex, the Airport Catering site (**colour plate 13**), Stansted, are perhaps the best medium for showing what this type of Iron Age settlement looked like. Usually in excavation reports only the plan of the site (for example at Winnal Down in Hampshire) is used to show the layout of the sites, the ditches, round house and the distribution of selected artefacts.

82 *Quarley Hill near Danebury, Hampshire. A hillfort with associated linear ditches which define an area without smaller fields but which may be contemporary with the small rectangular fields in the west* (Crown Copyright RCHME).

The settlement history at Winnal Down goes back to the Neolithic, with an open settlement in the Bronze Age, which is replaced in the Early Iron Age by a D-shaped enclosure; the ditch of the enclosure was partially filled in the middle Iron Age and an open settlement established. Winnal Down was unlikely to have been a high-status site and could be described, like Thorpe Thewles, as the average Iron Age settlement. There is evidence for metalworking in the late phases, there are a few items of ornament and wealth but nothing exceptional. The wealth of its occupants will have been derived from woollen goods and livestock in the early Iron Age (as there seems to be some evidence for textiles), and from cereal production in the middle Iron Age.

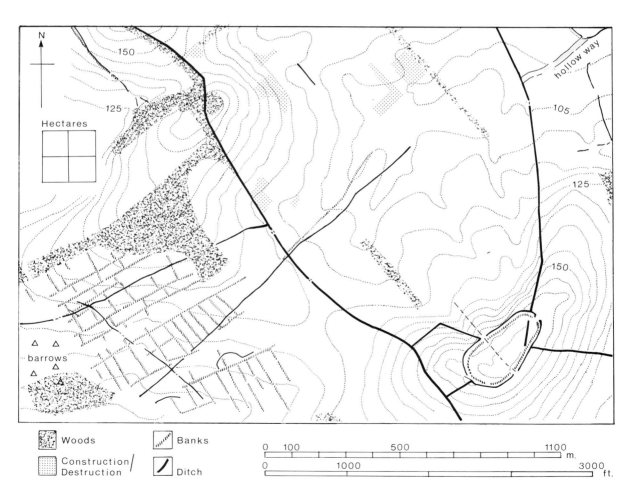

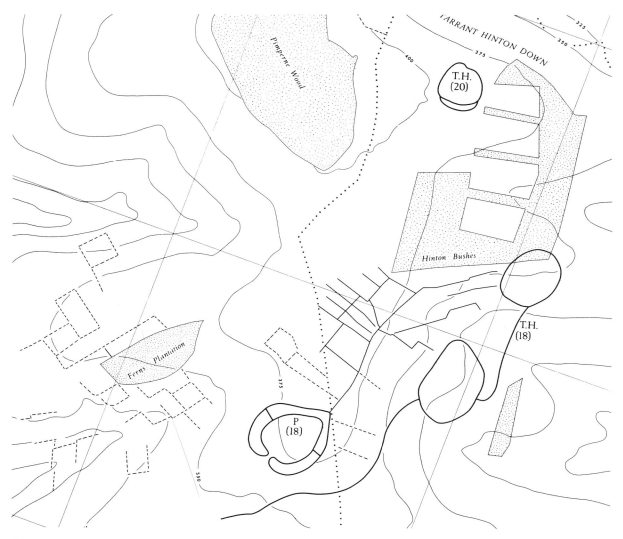

83 *Pimperne, Dorset. The excavated site is the one labelled T.H. (18), see aerial photograph below. Note the juxtaposition of other sites and field systems* (Crown Copyright RCHME).

Mention of Pimperne has already been made (**64**), and it is worth returning to the site and landscape around Pimperne. Survey work had revealed a landscape on the chalk which includes sites with which we are familiar (**83**) and also the more unusual (**84**). This site seems to be a developed form of the double-ditched enclosure with divisions in the outer enclosure; this may be to meet a particular need or

function and seems to be related to cattle or stock control.

Through aerial photography archaeologists have been discovering new sites – some of which are inevitably threatened, as is the one near Ashton Keynes, Wiltshire (**colour plate 10**), it being so near gravel pits (though fortunately it is 'scheduled', which means it is protected from total destruction by law) – but also new classes of site. In Wales, Terry James has discovered a whole new class of site, which he has called

84 *Aerial photograph of Pimperne 18, Dorset* (Crown Copyright RCHME, ST 9110/41).

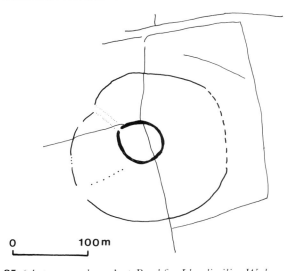

0   100m

85 *'Antenna enclosure' at Brechfa, Llandissilio, Wales, a new class of site; the 'antenna' is the outer ring (after Terry James).*

'concentric antenna enclosures' which are presumed to be Iron Age in date (**85**).

Perhaps a more familiar site, still in Wales, is a quadruple-ditched enclosure, at Collfryn (**86**), with a series of Iron Age (and later) hut circles (**87**); this site is one of many semi-defensive enclosures in the upper Severn valley in mid-Wales. The first enclosure was built in the third century BC and may have consisted of three encircling ditches, with a single entrance. From the finds it is likely to have been a reasonably high-status site with an extended-family group. At this time there was probably 3–4 roundhouses and 4–5 four-posters at any

86 *Collfryn, Wales, defended enclosure from the air* (copyright: Clywd Powys Archaeological Trust).

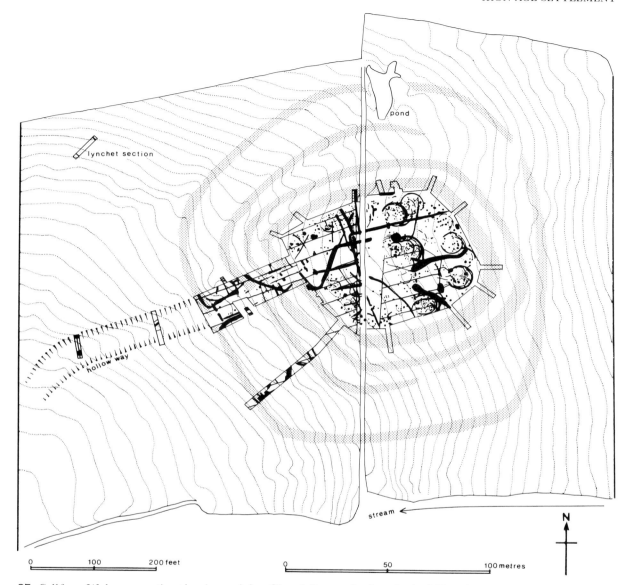

87 *Collfryn, Wales, excavation plan* (copyright: Clwyd-Powys Archaeological Trust).

one time. The site was reduced in the first century BC to a double-ditched enclosure by re-cutting the original inner ditch and digging a new one immediately outside it. There was a mixed farming economy of cattle, sheep (or goat) and pig remains with remains of glume wheats, barley and oats. Self-sufficiency was required in most daily needs including the making of bronze and iron tools. Pottery was rare in this area (as it was in the north of England in the

Iron Age). Small-scale occupation at the site continued until the fourth century AD. This type of site was obviously a 'defended' farmstead, though what the defences were is debated.

The concept of families defending and enclosing their homes begins in the late second millennium and continues throughout the rest of prehistoric Britain into the medieval period (moats and defended manor houses, for example).

IMPRESSION OF STAPLE HOWE IN THE LAST STAGE OF OCCUPATION

88 *Staple Howe, north Yorkshire. Situated on the northern edge of the Yorkshire Wolds, overlooking the Vale of Pickering. First excavated in May 1951 having been discovered by chance when four people were picnicking on the site. The small knoll was encircled by a timber palisade, with 2 round houses and a granary inside.*

A good example of this is the settlement at Staple Howe (**88**), a small farmstead in the latter part of the sixth century BC; the site occupied a natural knoll and was enclosed by a palisade. Initially the site contained an oval hut which was later replaced by two round huts. The pottery has close affinities with Holland, Belgium and France and the excavator suggested that the inhabitants embarked from the mouth of the Rhine and settled at Staple Howe. This is a superb concept that we have the initial settlement of the first settlers, but the evidence does not support it. The pottery, although imported, has been found on earlier sites elsewhere in Yorkshire. They ate ox, goat, sheep, pig, red and roe deer, fish and wheat.

The site catchment included three areas – the high chalk of the Wolds, the long wide 'low' wet valley of the vale of Pickering, and the vale of York to the south and west, all of which would have been rich in natural resources.

Brochs, duns and crannogs

As we move further north the sites in Scotland have been referred to in the Bronze Age but the first millennium BC in Scotland can be characterised by crannogs, brochs and duns. Brochs are the most visually striking and relatively common. The aerial photograph of the broch of Gurness (**colour plate 16**) shows the broch itself (the remains of the tower which might have been 12m (37ft) high). Figure **89** (Dun Telve) shows the internal construction of the broch, with a staircase to the upper floors. Brochs were probably roofed, and each floor level properly spanned. They would have been dark inside but they had lamps. The broch was encircled by three lines of ditch and rampart with an entrance to the east. The broch (which was one aspect of the Iron Age 'settlement') is surrounded by stone-built houses which date from a later period, but which may have been built on earlier houses. Once again the siting of the broch on the edge of a low cliff overlooking the sea emphasises the importance of the sea to the prehistoric communities. The study of the location of brochs and the subject of 'broch-ology' is undergoing a revival but the work of Sir Lindsay Scott in the 1940s showed that the brochs were situated to command an area of farmland which was moderately large by modern farm standards but small given the quality of soil.

Brochs and duns in Scotland have been characterised by topographical location and architectural style, and not in terms of how they function as settlement systems within the economic strategies of the Iron Age. New evidence is coming to light from recent excavations that the people who lived in the brochs all used similar material cultural items but that their diet was less consistent. This latter diversity has led to the suggestion that the inhabitants of the brochs were of a higher status than other Iron Age communities.

One item studied is the wall width in proportion to height; the thicker the wall the higher the broch. To achieve the same floor area (thin low building, or high thick building) thicker walls would be needed. More floors would have allowed for greater flexibility of use; animal stalling, storage, and living areas.

Duns are related to brochs in that they are stone-built and are often in similar locatons. If you look at any OS map of Scotland you will see the coastal cliff edges and hill tops littered with the gothic writing *dun*. Even those with the same shape and size have different functions because of location. Those near good land will have functioned differently from those on exposed cliff-edges.

The view that brochs and duns can be seen as regional variants in the Atlantic culture stone-building tradition (and not a chronological sequence) is expressed well at the sites of

89 *Internal structure of Dun Telve broch* (copyright: Professor DW Harding).

Dun Trodan, Dun Telve (brochs) and Dun Grugaig (dun or semi-broch) in Glen Beag (in north-west Scotland on the way to Skye). Their location is determined by the proximity of good agricultural land. The same point is noted by Mercer about brochs in Hallidale (Caithness) and by Stevenson about duns in Tiree. Ian Morrison in his book on crannogs has also noted that in Loch Awe crannogs do not occur opposite the land which is good for grazing and has a dun situated near it.

121

90 *Reconstruction of a crannog from a number of surveys and excavation (*drawn by Jean Williamson*).*

Crannogs (**90**) are an important part of the prehistoric settlement pattern. They are not only ubiquitous but they also contain water-logged organic material, which when excavated reveals much more about the prehistoric way of life than the material from dry-land sites. The drawback with crannogs is their inaccessibility. They are usually situated in the middle of a lake, loch or expanse of water.

The term crannog comes from a Gaelic word *crannag*, or in Irish *crannog*; and the *crann*-element in the word implies 'wood'. As with so many terms they have been accepted as common usage even though a crannog may also refer to uninhabited or totally unaltered islands in lochs and loughs. There has been an increase in the work done on them but there is much more that could be studied. Brochs, duns and crannogs should not be studied as isolated monument classes but as part of an integrated landscape pattern so that more information is obtained about their date, function and distribution.

Glastonbury Lake Village
Research on crannogs in England and Wales has not been as fruitful as in Scotland and there is scope for work in the Lake District and the lakes in Wales. There is one site which, although on dry (drained) land now, might have been

similar to crannogs two thousand years ago. The Glastonbury Lake Village is one of the most studied and re-examined of all the Iron Age sites in England (**91; colour plate 14**), and one with good preservation.

Over 100 years have elapsed since the discoveries and excavations by Arthur Bulleid began at Glastonbury Lake Village in 1892. In the introduction to the excavation report (published in 1911), Munro said: 'In the course

of a couple of years the fame of the Glastonbury Lake Village became so great that people flocked from all parts of the country to the site of this singular dwelling place.' It is interesting to note that between 1892 and 1907 a total of £92 18s 6d was collected for 'Entrance fees to the Field'; if we knew how much each person had been charged we could work out the number of paying visitors. It is likely to have been less than sixpence each; if it was threepence each approximately 7434 people would have visited. In the days before cars, tarmac roads and the great 'heritage industry' this is a considerable number of people, even if it is wrong by a factor of two!

91 *Glastonbury Lake Village. Plan of the mounds and palisade (dotted line), and the extent of the excavated area* (after Bullied, Coles and Coles).

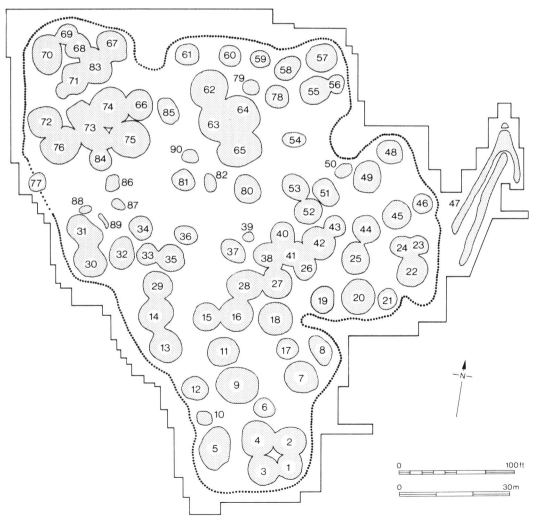

The site was discovered by Arthur Bulleid and has 90 or more low mounds and the whole area was excavated; the site plan (**91**) reveals the complexity of the mounds. The complexity of the site has warranted a number of interpretations and analyses.

David Clarke, an exponent of archaeological theory, proposed a model for each 'unit' of occupation; this model has had its critics (because of its lack of reality) but it is possible to argue that the very existence of the model helped the recent re-interpretations emerge in the way that they did.

Clarke's model attempts to say that there is a modular unit (like a portacabin approach to Iron Age villages) which comprised two sorts of houses in which the major houses and their satellites and the minor house and its ancillaries are divided between 'a major familial, multi-role and activity area on the one hand and a minor, largely female and domestic area'.

Clarke defines seven structural types (I–VII) which are repeatedly reproduced on the site; he interprets this as 'a particular transformation of an otherwise standardized set of relationships between the structural category and every other category'. If I understand this correctly, the suggestion is that throughout the 90 or so mounds at Glastonbury a repeated, standard 'household type' would be found; moreover this building block is also reflected in the total plan for the whole site. The model is thus a reflection of each household area and the whole site. This may be an interesting theory and provoke some discussion but is it anywhere near the truth?

The latest re-interpretation has been by John Coles whose work in the Somerset Levels has shown the close relationship prehistoric peoples had with wet, boggy bits of land which modern (post-sixteenth century) land-use activities drain at an alarming rate. Having worked for so long in the Somerset Levels, John Coles has turned his attention to a re-interpretation of the Glastonbury Lake Village. Apart from completely re-working the theoretical model his scheme also provides a chronological frame-work for the site. There are four phases for the occupation at Glastonbury. The Early phase which comprised a few hut circles and several sheds, dated around 150 BC; in this phase the platform building began. In the Middle phase the settlement expanded, with new houses being built, a couple of which burnt down, and the palisade around the crannog was started. There was further expansion in the Late phase, with a number of new structures and the completion of the palisade. In the Final contraction phase there were only a few houses occupied, and the site was finally abandoned in AD 50.

This sequence would have seen several families living at the Glastonbury Lake Village in 150 BC, perhaps 70 people in all; this would have expanded to 200 people in the peak (Late phase) with a reduction in numbers in the Final phase to about 100 people. There is the possibility that one or two houses were for the ruling elite, perhaps reserved for the chieftain and his (or her) family.

There would have been satellite farms and settlements which may well have made up a Glastonbury hamlet, but these have not been discovered. There is another Lake village at Meare (6km, 3.75 miles, west of Glastonbury), also excavated by Bullied and Gray once they had finished work at Glastonbury. Here there are two groups of mounds which were the remains of a late Iron Age village. It has been argued that this site was a summer meeting place for all Iron Age communities around, and unlike Glastonbury Lake Village was seasonally occupied.

The communities at Glastonbury had a well-balanced food supply consisting of peas, barley, wheat, spelt, pig, and fish. The discovery of small sickles suggest that the crop was cut below the ear leaving the stalks for pasture; grazing for the sheep was necessary as the wool was probably used for more than local needs. The flocks of sheep would perhaps have been wintered in the highlands with summer grazing in the lower, wetter areas. The faunal assemblage also reveals the presence of all types of birds;

92 *Sutton Common, south Yorkshire. Aerial photograph of two enclosures which excavations have shown contain Neolithic to Iron Age material; they are now threatened by ploughing and drainage* (courtesy of Derrick Riley).

the list is quite exhaustive in the excavation report – cormorant, heron, bittern, puffin, swan, pelican, teal, golden eye, pintail, shoveller, wigeon, tufted duck, scaup, pochard, red-breasted merganser, coot, crane, little grebe, sea eagle, goshawk, kite, barn owl, and carrion crow. The local environment near to the settlement was marsh and mere. Many of the birds would have been killed by clay pellets from a sling; some of the birds were very young (pelican, swan and crane) and the evidence is that they were breeding locally. Fish, too, will have formed an important component of the diet, probably roach, trout, shad, and perch.

There is also good evidence for metalworking, spinning, pottery manufacture, wood working, basket making, weaving and comb manufacture. There are also dice for gambling, and cock spurs for cock fighting.

Glastonbury Lake Village will always remain one of the unique sites in British prehistory not least for its preservation and total excavation; its position in the wet peatlands of the Somerset Levels should make the discovery of a site in a similar position in South Yorkshire less of a surprise. Aerial photography by the late Derrick Riley, a pioneer of aerial photography, discovered this site (**92**); recent excavations have shown these two enclosures to be unique in terms of shape but a now familiar story of well preserved deposits drying out. The deposits contain material from the Mesolithic through to the Iron Age but the bank and ditches as seen now are of an Iron Age date. Unless the draining and ploughing is stopped this site will be destroyed; it is included here as a tribute to the work of Derrick Riley who first started

93 *'I expect you've heard about Roman roads'*

recording crop marks in the Thames Valley in the 1930s and continued working, worldwide, until 1993.

Oppida

It is easier for us to comprehend the way of life of Iron Age sites – hillforts, farmsteads, enclosed sites, open farms or villages – as they are not too distant from our own experience. There were, however, developments at the end of the Iron Age and at the beginning of the Roman period that are akin to early town development and should be even more familiar.

Often the classical authors referred to some of the settlements in Britain as *oppida* (Caesar referred to the defended sites in Gaul as *oppida*). Suetonius in his *Life of Vespasian* mentions that Vespasian captured the Isle of Wight and 20 *oppida*; surely this means some of the hillforts of southern England.

Strictly speaking *oppidum* means 'town', but Maiden Castle would have been seen as a town to a visiting Roman. There is, however, a class of site in European archaeology called *oppida*, which usually refers to large urban sites where size and organisation and not defence are the basic defining criteria. In Britain the usage is less clear and strictly the main *oppida* would have been Colchester and St Albans where the large size, low-ground siting and linear dykes (sort of town walls) set them apart from defended hillforts.

John Collis, who has written a book on *oppida*, favours a definition which has defence as an element in the definition but this must be combined with the internal use, i.e. a town worth defending. Although in European terms *oppida* are important in the development of towns there are probably only a few examples in southern England which meet the criteria. Roman towns developed partly as a result of the existing Iron Age system but were more

126

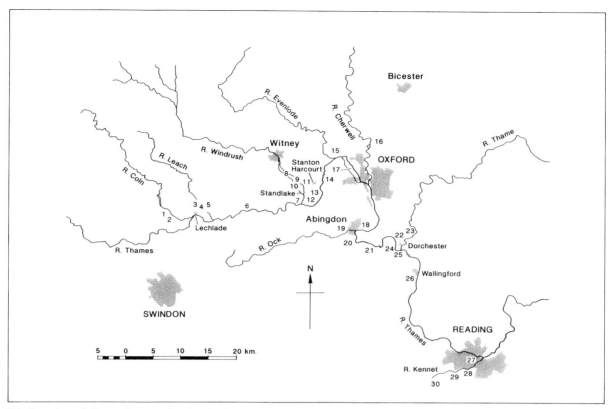

94 *Location of sites and excavation by the Oxford Archaeological Unit in the Thames Valley* (copyright: Oxford Archaeological Unit).

influenced by the Roman military geography of Britannia (**93**).

Other landscapes

In moving through the prehistoric settlements by period (Mesolithic to the Iron Age) there was little time to explore certain landscapes which are either so diverse that they cannot be fitted neatly into one time band, or they are so specific and self-contained yet undated that they do not easily fall into any scheme. This section briefly covers these two extremes. The former in this instance is the Thames Valley and the latter a small island off the west coast of Wales, Skomer Island.

The Thames Valley, from Gloucestershire in the west to London (**94**) in the east, contains archaeological deposits of all periods from the Palaeolithic to the Industrial Revolution.

Recently it has been the focus of survey and excavation brought about by changes in agriculture since 1945, the development of aerial photography and the need for gravel for all types of construction projects (houses and roads in particular). The crop-mark evidence of all the river gravels in Britain has been known about since the seminal work by the RCHME, *A Matter of Time*, was published in 1960. This presented an encouraging picture of the wealth of archaeology in gravel areas and a gloomy forecast for the rate of destruction. New sites are discovered each year (**colour plates 1, 10**) and more areas are excavated as the gravel pits inexorably expand. There is not the space here to summarise 40 years' work but for prehistoric settlement there has been an increase in our knowledge of the area; the gloomy forecast of 1960 has been proved correct in that many

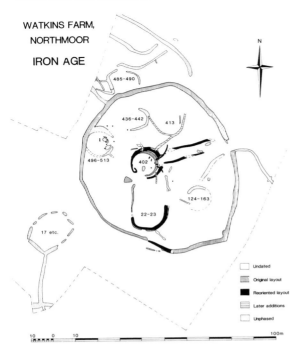

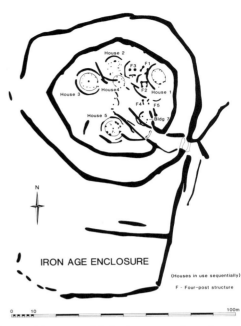

95 *Excavation plan of the Iron Age enclosures at Watkins Farm and Mingies Ditches* (copyright: Oxford Archaeological Unit).

archaeological sites have been destroyed, and the number excavated represents a small percentage of what has been destroyed.

The Thames Valley itself has been overworked in comparison to the study of land-use and settlement on the valley slopes. A biased picture is emerging which has little to do with what actually went on in the past. This is partly determined by our own land-use in which arable cultivation has led to discoveries of crop marks in river gravels. These sites are also threatened because of our own need for gravel. Crop marks reveal important sites but in river valleys there can be a negative correlation between the clarity of the crop mark and preservation: thinner soils produce clearer marks because the buried features are nearer the surface but might have been plough-damaged; crop marks beneath alluvium are often faint, but preservation is better.

On the evidence which is emerging from river gravels the population density in the Roman period is argued to have been equal to that of Middle Ages. The explosion of the population began in late Iron Age with the intensification of agriculture. In the Bronze Age the settlement pattern in the middle Thames Valley was based on the need for herding livestock although there was some arable activity. Paddocks and wells are absent from early Iron Age sites which suggests arable was the predominant form of agriculture and not cattle. In the middle Iron Age these features come back suggesting a more mixed farming approach, including horse rearing.

George Lambrick has identified three types of site:

1 'Banjo' enclosures, Mingies Ditch and Watkins Farm (**95**), ditched and hedged farms with funnel shaped entrances and areas for coralling livestock with pens and paddocks.

2 Open settlements such as Claydon Pike, Port Meadow, and perhaps Gill Mill (**96**),

with paddocks – on dry ground within the alluvial floodplain. These were in use for a long time as there are at least two phases of layout.

3 Small one-phase farmsteads, revealed beneath the alluvial deposits, seasonal and short-lived which specialized pastoralism in the middle Iron Age. The Farmoor settlement is a good example. There would have been summer grazing on the floodplain and the location of settlement dictated by land

96 *The area near Stanton Harcourt in the Thames Valley showing the relationship of prehistoric sites with each other and the different geologies* (copyright: Oxford Archaeological Unit).

use. In the Stanton Harcourt area it is now possible to suggest that a series of mixed farms on the second terrace may have formed part of a single community with a variety of pastoral farmsteads on the lower ground, the whole complex occupying the equivalent of about two modern parishes.

In the late Iron Age, at Barton Court Farm, there is evidence of the intensification of arable, the growing of bread wheats, but also horticulture with deeper ploughing on heavier soils and better drainage. This assisted the onset of alluviation if poorer valley slopes soils were being ploughed. There appears to have been an increase in enclosure of fields, some probably quite large; manuring was taking place, given the

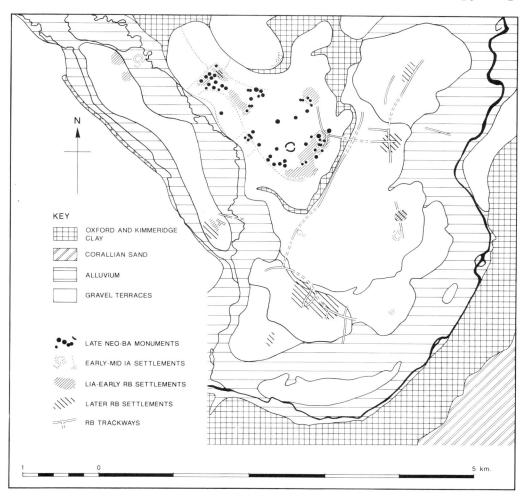

scatters of pottery found during fieldwalking. From the research by the Oxford Unit, George Lambrick concludes that the importance of pastoralism is underplayed in the Iron Age. Even though arable production expanded, productivity did not increase (**96**); with the arrival of the Romans advances in tech-

nology and the introduction of new species had a real effect. In the late Iron Age and early Roman period the farms remained much the same in an unchanged landscape structure; the conquest of the Romans was invisible in the Thames Valley. This indicates an agricultural, social and economic system which was working well, was prosperous and not in any need of change. It also assumes a population willing to serve a new master, or was the master (the Romans) paying the right price?

The Thames Valley has been the subject of a huge amount of work over the last 30 years, with surveys and excavations, and recently a complete re-mapping of all the crop-mark evidence from aerial photographs by RCHME's Air Photography Unit. So often archaeologists are expected to provide *the* answer *now*; this can be achieved for a few specific questions. For the central, fundamental questions about sites or regions research takes a long time and it will be many years before we fully understand the archaeology of the Thames Valley.

This is well exemplified with the next example. In complete contrast to the length and complexity of the Thames Valley, is the small island off the west coast of Wales, Skomer Island. It is well known for its wildlife, especially birdlife (the largest colony of Manx shearwaters in the world). The island was first archaeologically recorded by Professor Grimes in the 1950s. More recently, under the supervision of Dr John Evans of Cardiff University the island's archaeology has been mapped and recorded by students; aerial photographs helped in locating and identifying sites (**97**). The system of field walls and settlements is clearly visible and a visit to the island is worthwhile; time your visit so that the archaeology will be visible (the bracken obscures the archaeology from June onwards) – but beware of the birds!

In the reports on the field survey it is clear that something is known about the settlements, and the field pattern, even damming water. There is even the suggestion that two of the features are 'saunas'; there is a growing amount of evidence that 'sweat boxes' were used in prehistory from a number of sites. This removes us further from the filthy savage idea of our ancestors. The major problem with the Skomer landscape is that we know so little about it in terms of who lived there (an estimate has been between 100 and 200 people at any one time), and why was it abandoned? What was the date and length of occupation? John Evans in his short guide (*Prehistoric Farmers of Skomer Island*) argues that the occupation was short-lived, as there is little evidence of the fields being sub-divided or extended. We do not know its date, but it is typical of later prehistoric settlement in the west of Britain; what makes Skomer unique is the survival of the almost complete system of a prehistoric farming community.

To experience what life must have been like in prehistory is impossible but by visiting places like Skomer, the western Isles of Scotland and Orkney (to name just a few) it is possible to experience a flavour of the environment in which they lived. The high bird population, especially migratory species must have been an important food resource; if the bird populations are high now what must they have been like 3000 years ago?

7
Conclusions

Archaeology is a combination of obtaining information, interpreting, analysing, and then modelling new and old evidence; as a subject it is always changing.

A major theme of prehistoric archaeology is the changes which take place over thousands of years. The landscape is ever-changing either as a result of human interference or because of the global changes which have taken place in the last 8000 years. Similarly human adaptation to a whole range of factors (social, ritual, environmental, and ecological) changes through time. This results in a kaleidoscopic picture and makes the study of prehistoric settlements both frustrating and challenging. It is the reason why there are no absolute answers to the questions about social organisation and settlement pattern.

The theme of interpretation and re-interpretation is also part of the kaleidoscope. Inevitably our knowledge of prehistoric settlements will increase, and interpretations will develop. To allow this to happen we have to be aware of the different scales at which prehistoric people and twentieth-century society operate. Often the scale can be defined in distances, or in expectations. The example of Dartmoor as a central place in prehistory but considered marginal today is a good example.

The fact that we discuss long-distance trade in the Neolithic reflects that prehistoric people travelled very long distances. We travel long distances today but we expect to travel hundreds of miles in a day, whereas travelling the same distance might have been a seasonal activity or on a yearly or five-yearly cycle in prehistory.

Similarly, if we consider the daily experience of living in a prehistoric settlement and their 'world', the scale is significant. For hunters, gatherers or farmers an intricate knowledge of the very local area would have been a prerequisite for survival of the community. The challenge which faces archaeology is the way in which we study the interrelationship of sites in any area. We need to know the contemporaneity of sites, the hierarchy of sites, and we need to examine the function of sites. So often we have only the midden, the rubbish dump, on which to build our theories. These are important biases to our understanding of prehistoric communities; it is difficult to understand any human community if we only rely on what they left behind.

Likewise, the techniques of recovery are biased. Aerial photography is one aspect which has helped the study of prehistoric settlements, but it is not without its limitations. Recent work in the Thames Valley has shown that there are large areas of crop marks, but that the other – supposedly blank – areas contain as much, if not more information when excavated. I have made liberal use of aerial photographs to illustrate the sites mentioned in this book, but their major use is in providing information for maps which contain archaeological information. At the appropriate scale the maps will be useful in studying the distribution of sites, but they can also help to preserve sites, by providing the information in a usable form to the appropriate body. Modern archaeology is as much about understanding the past as it is about preserving the fragile remains, and aerial photography has been a significant factor in these two aspects.

Chris Taylor argued in 1972 that the present rate of destruction of archaeological sites was so fast that by AD 2000 there would be nothing left for archaeologists to do. In 1972 the end of the millennium must have seemed a generation away; today it is only a 'corporate plan' away. Surveys are going on continuously in Britain, by the Royal Commissions, Archaeological Units and Trusts and county archaeologists. There is a programme for England (being undertaken by RCHME) to map all the archaeological sites seen on aerial photographs; this will take all concerned well into the next century and even then we will only be beginning to know the full (knowable) extent of the prehistoric archaeology of England. The continuing surveys in Scotland, Wales and Ireland will complete the picture for the rest of Britain.

The study of archaeology is the study of change, which is sometimes referred to as progess. Technologically there may have been progress in the development of sophisticated computers and machinery, but socially has anything changed in the last 8000 years? As a species we are still learning to live together (or not live together) in towns and cities, or in isolated communities. Throughout prehistory and history there has been conflict between human communities and this aspect of human behaviour is represented in the archaeological record for prehistoric settlements.

The extent to which we interpret, or emphasise, any particular aspect of prehistory will be a function of our own background and beliefs.

Sites to Visit

A short list of archaeological guides is listed under Further Reading. If you have no restraints on your time and a complete set of Ordnance Survey 1:50,000 Landranger maps for the whole country, you can happily spend years visiting every site marked as an antiquity. Many of these sites are settlements or field systems; even if they are burial mounds, henges or stone circles at least you will be visiting places of prehistoric interest. The OS map *Ancient Britain*, also provides a very good introduction to prehistoric sites in Britain.

Many of the sites are on private land and permission must be obtained prior to any visit. Public footpaths often run near or through many of the sites and some of these paths are marked on the Landranger maps.

Northern England

Carrock Fell   The most dramatic setting for a stone-built hillfort in northern Cumbria. The steep climb up from east is well worth the effort. 6km (3.75 miles) SSE of Caldbeck.

Castle Crag   An imposing setting for a small fort with two rock-cut ditches overlooking Mardale (now Haweswater Reservoir) in Cumbria.

Crosby Ravensworth   A series of settlements surviving as earthworks to the south, south-east and west of the village of Crosby Ravensworth, Cumbria dating to the prehistoric and Roman periods. Survey plans were published in the *Inventory for Westmorland*, RCHME (1936) 78–92.

Eston Nab   This hillfort overlooks the industrial heart of Middlesbrough but is a reminder of the changes which have taken place in the last 3000 years. SE of Middlesbrough, S of the A174.

Great Urswick, Cumbria   An Iron Age hillfort on a limestone plateau with perhaps earlier remains. 4km (2.5 miles) SSE of Ulverston.

Ingleborough   One of the highest hillforts in England. Remains of hut circles with stone foundations and a stone rampart. Possibly one of the strongholds of the Brigantes tribe, situated on the top of a plateau in the centre of the Pennines (**back cover**).

Ingram Valley, Northumberland   An area of well preserved settlements and field systems on either side of the Beamish river. Most are on private land, but those which are accessible via a public footpath are marked on the Landranger Map no. 81. 16km (10 miles) NNW of Rothbury.

Mam Tor, Derbyshire   The impressive position and ramparts of this hillfort make it a favourite location for walkers and hang gliders. Inside the ramparts are numerous platforms presumably for huts and houses; there is evidence of earlier Bronze Age material on the site.

Yeavering, Northumberland Stone-built hillfort with hut circles, a round cairn and extra-mural terraces. Very commanding position on the top of a steeply rising fell, Yeavering Bell. The hillfort overlooks the Millfield Basin, an area rich in prehistoric archaeology and two Anglo-Saxon royal palaces.

Yorkshire Dales Numerous settlements and field systems especially around Grassington, but elsewhere throughout the Yorkshire Dales National Park. Further information can be obtained from the local National Park Offices in Grassington and from the Landranger maps.

Southern England

Bodbury Ring, Shropshire A small triangular hillfort with very steep approaches and commanding a strategic position in these border lands. Access is via the Church Stretton golf course.

Butser Ancient Farm A reconstruction of an Iron Age farm, with large and small round houses, industrial working areas, fields with crops, sheep and cattle. Near Chalton, Hampshire (**colour plate 11**). For further information telephone 0705 598838.

Carn Brea, Cornwall The largest Iron Age hillfort in Cornwall of 18ha (46 acres) with hut circles inside. The eastern summit has revealed evidence of Neolithic occupation.

Carn Euny, Cornwall Iron Age to Romano-British hamlet, with three interlocking courtyard houses and other round houses. Within the settlement is a well-preserved fogou.

Castle an Dinas, Cornwall A well-preserved Iron Age hillfort with three ramparts and an earlier Bronze Age cairn.

Chysauster, Cornwall The best preserved example of a courtyard house hamlet, only one mile east of Castle an Dinas hillfort. The visible remains are Romano-British but there is good evidence for the earlier settlement (**colour plate 15**).

Crickley Hill, Gloucestershire Originally a Neolithic causewayed camp but developing into an Iron Age promontory fort dating from the sixth century BC. Now part of a Country Park it is a good place for a day out or picnic. Stunning views overlooking the Vale of Gloucester.

Danebury, Hampshire This is one of the few Iron Age hillforts to have been extensively excavated. In the Bronze Age the summit was marked by a number of ritual pits. The first Iron Age hillfort was constructed in fifth century BC and it underwent four major redevelopments before finally being abandoned some time after the arrival of the Romans (**80**).

Dartmoor, Devon The Dartmoor landscape, especially the reave system, has to be experienced and this can be achieved by walking through its moors and valleys. Individual sites can be selected by looking at the Landranger maps, but Grimspound and the Rider's Rings (see below) are two accessible sites (**41**).

Flag Fen Visitor Centre, Cambs Excavations of Bronze Age wooden structures and reconstructions of a Bronze Age Lake Village and round houses. Educational guided tours are available. For further information ring 0733 313414 (**colour plate 7**).

Grimspound, Devon A stone-built Bronze Age settlement on the east side of Dartmoor. Within the stone walls are numerous hut circles and cattle pens.

Hambledon Hill, Dorset This long ridge contains the remains of a Neolithic causewayed camp and an enormous Iron Age hillfort. Research and excavation have shown that the causewayed camp was abandoned after being attacked. The hillfort developed and expanded to its present size during the Iron Age (cf. Maiden Castle, (**29**)).

Hod Hill, Dorset One of the largest hillforts to be taken by Vespasian in AD 43. The Iron Age hillfort contains a Roman fort in its north-western corner (**68, 72**). (Visit Hambledon Hill at the same time.)

Maiden Castle, Dorset Comparable to Hambledon Hill in that a Neolithic causewayed camp is contained within a multi-vallate hillfort. Excavations have taken place twice during this century and the hillfort developed to be one of the largest and most important in southern England during the Iron Age (**7**).

Rider's Rings, Devon A Bronze Age stone-built settlement comprising two enclosures or pounds which contain numerous huts and possible stock pens (**42**).

Rough Tor, Cornwall On this summit there are a number of oval enclosures with hut circles which are the remains of Bronze Age and Iron Age settlements, possibly hillforts (**colour plate 5**).

Stowe's Pound, Cornwall The two stone enclosures on Stowe's Hill are of different sizes and are perhaps Neolithic in origin with occupation continuing into the Bronze Age. The larger encircles the summit and contains over 100 house platforms, the smaller oval enclosure is attached to the southern end of the larger hillfort (**colour plate 6**).

The Trundle, Sussex Neolithic causewayed camp and an octagonal Iron Age hillfort commanding views in all directions.

Windmill Hill, Wiltshire One of the first causewayed camps to be identified in the 1930s. With good access and numerous round barrows within the three encircling ditches, it is one of the classic sites in Wessex. Near Avebury and Silbury Hill (**26**).

Wales
Burfa Camp An impressive multi-vallate hillfort set within too many trees, but recent clearance has revealed the entrance more clearly.

Caerau Hillfort Near Ely, Cardiff in the east end of the Vale of Glamorgan, three ramparts surround a natural plateau to provide the setting of one of the strongest forts in South Wales.

Carn Goch A hillfort with a stone rampart enclosing 10ha (24 acres) in a very commanding position, 5km (3 miles) north-east of Llandeilo.

Tre'r Ceiri Known as the 'town of the giants' this stone-built hillfort encloses the summit of one of three hills overlooking the Lleyn peninsula and the coast. Within the ramparts are numerous stone huts. In the Roman period an outer rampart was added, more huts were built and the earlier huts re-modelled (**73**).

Scotland
Broch of Gurness, Orkney This broch is one of the most impressive in Britain. The tower would have originally stood 12m (37ft) high. The stone-built settlement surrounding the tower will have had Iron Age origins but as visible today represent first millennium AD houses (**colour plate 16**).

Dun Carloway, Lewis One of the best preserved brochs in Scotland, containing typical broch features such as two side cells leading off the courtyard.

Dun Telve, Lochalsh With only part of the wall of this broch standing it is possible to see the internal broch structure. There are a number of stone outbuildings which may have been stock pens (**89**).

Finavon, Angus A good example of vitrified (stones fused by heat) fort. The ramparts are over 6m (20ft) thick and were probably timber laced.

Jarslhof, Shetland Occupation at this stone-built settlement site began in the Bronze Age and continued until the seventeenth century AD. The prehistoric settlement consists of round and oval houses and workshops.

137

Mousa Broch, Shetland With the tower standing 13m (46ft) this broch is the best-preserved in Britain; at its base the tower is 15m (50ft) in diameter.

Skara Brae, Orkney Neolithic village with a group of interconnecting stone-built houses. One of the most famous sites of British prehistory and situated on the coast it is well worth a visit (**31**).

Woden Law, Roxburghshire A strategic setting for a hillfort which continued its influence into the Roman period as it commanded the area close to Dere Street, the Roman road from York to the Firth of Forth (**55**).

Further Reading

Archaeological Guides

Dyer, James, *Southern England: An Archaeological Guide*, Faber, London, 1973

Houlder, Christopher, *Wales: An Archaeological Guide*, Faber, London, 1978

MacSween, Ann and Sharp, Mick, *Prehistoric Scotland*, Batsford, London, 1989

Cornwall Archaeological Unit, *Cornwall's Archaeological Heritage*, Twelveheads, Truro, 1990

Cornwall Archaeological Unit, *Scilly's Archaeological Heritage*, Twelveheads, Truro, 1992

Ritchie, Anna and Graham Ritchie, *The Ancient Monuments of Orkney*, Historic Scotland, HMSO, Edinburgh, 1990

General Reading

Audouze, Françoise and Büchenschütz, Olivier, *Towns, Villages and Countryside of Celtic Europe*, Batsford, London, 1989

Bradley, Richard, *The Prehistoric Settlement of Britain*, Routledge, Kegan and Paul, London, 1978

Burgess, Colin, *The Age of Stonehenge*, J. M. Dent, London, 1980

Coles, Bryony and John Coles, *Sweet Track to Glastonbury: the Somerset Levels in Prehistory*, Thames & Hudson, London, 1986

Cunliffe, Barry, *Iron Age Communities in Britain*, Routledge, Kegan and Paul, London, 1975 (new ed. 1993)

Darvill, Tim, *Prehistoric Britain*, Batsford, London, 1987

Dyer, James, *Hillforts of England and Wales*, Shire Archaeology, Princes Risborough, 1992

Fleming, Andrew, *The Dartmoor Reaves: Investigating Prehistoric Land Divisions*, Batsford, London, 1988

Fowler, Peter, *The Farming of Prehistoric Britain*, Cambridge University Press, Cambridge, 1983

Hogg, A.H.A, *British Hill-Forts: An Index*, British Archaeological Reports 62, Oxford, 1978

Lubbock, John, *Pre-historic Times*, Williams and Norgate, London, 1865

Mercer, Roger, *Causewayed Enclosures*, Shire Archaeology, Princes Risborough, 1990

Mellars, Paul (ed.), *The Early Postglacial Settlement of Northern Europe*, Duckworth, London, 1978

Norfolk Museums Service, *Norfolk from the Air*, Norfolk Museum Service, Norwich, 1987

O'Kelly, Michael, *Early Ireland*, Cambridge University Press, Cambridge, 1989

Piggot, Stuart, *William Stukeley. An 18th century Antiquary*, Thames and Hudson, London, 1985

Renfrew, Colin, *British Prehistory: a new outline*, Duckworth, London, 1974

Riley, Derrick, *Aerial Archaeology in Britain*, Shire Archaeology, Princes Risborough, 1982

Wilson, David, *Air Photo Interpretation for Archaeologists*, Batsford, London, 1982

Related books in the Batsford/English Heritage series

Cunliffe, Barry, *Danebury*, 1993

Parker Pearson, Mike, *Bronze Age Britain*, 1993

Pryor, Francis, *Flag Fen: Prehistoric Fenland Centre*, 1991

Sharples, Niall, *Maiden Castle*, 1991

Useful Addresses

The Prehistoric Society, founded in 1935 is the only national body concerned exclusively with the study of prehistory. It has over 2000 members and provides its membership with a regular newsletter, *PAST*, an annual *Proceedings of the Prehistoric Society*, Study Tours and Conferences. For more information write to the Prehistoric Society, University College London, Institute of Archaeology, 31–34 Gordon Square, London WC1H 0PY.

Cambridge University Committee for Aerial Photography (CUCAP). The Mond Building, Free School Lane, Cambridge, CB2 3RF. Tel: 0223 334578. Fax: 0223 334400. The Collection may be visited by members of the public during normal office hours. Photographs cannot be borrowed but prints can be purchased; orders ordinarily take about a month. Prices depend on print size from £3.06 for a 5″ × 5″ black and white to £11.75 for 9″ × 9″ colour positives. Copyright is retained by the University or the Crown.

English Heritage. Fortress House, 23 Savile Row, London, W1X 1AB. Tel: 071 973 3000.

RCHME   The Royal Commission on the Historical Monuments of England. NMRC, Kemble Drive, Swindon SN2 2GZ. The national body for archaeological and architectural survey and record in England.

RCAHMW   The Royal Commission on the Ancient and Historical Monuments of Wales. Crown Buildings, Plas Crug, Aberystwyth, Dyfed SY23 2HP. The national body of survey and record for Wales.

RCAHMS   The Royal Commission on the Ancient and Historical Monuments of Scotland. John Sinclair House, 16 Bernard Terrace, Edinburgh EH8 9NX. The national body of survey and record for Scotland.

Index

(Numbers in **bold** refer to the figure number)

absolute dating methods 27
activity dispersal zones 35
aerial photographs 17, 22
aerial photography 17, 22, 93, 116, 124, 132
Air Photography Unit, RCHME 131
Airport Catering site 115, colour plate 13
alder 41
Algeria 65
alluviation 63
alluvium 80
Alyth Burn **56**, **57**, 87
Anatolia 57
Anglo-Saxon 62
animal bone 54
antiquarians 19
Antiquity 28
antler 39, 54
antler baton 56
apotropaic 56
archers 40
arrow 54
arrowheads 55, 65
Ashton Keynes 116, colour plate 10
astragalus 40
Atlantic 35
aurochs 37
Avebury 63, 101
axis mundi 59

badger 37
Balbridie **34**, 62–3
Balleygalley **33**, 60–1
Ballynagilly 62
Barfield Tarn **12**
barley 54, 63, 76, 119, 124
Barnhouse **32**, 57, 59, 64
barrow 51
Barton Court Farm 129
base camp 35
Beaker settlements 66
beakers 65, 67
beaver 37
beetles 30, 49
Behy-Glenurla 71
Belgium 120
Belle Tout **36**, 66

Belsar's Hill **71**
Bharpa Carinish 63
birch 41–2
birds 42, 59
bison 33
Black Patch **46**, **47**, **48**, 71, 77–9
Bodbury Ring 136
Bodmin Moor **37**, **38**, 67, 71, 75
Bodmin 15
bone assemblage 39
bow and arrow 37, 42
Bowmans Farm **20**, 42
bread wheat 129
Brechfa **85**, 118
Breiddin 94, 105
bristle-cone pine 28
British Isles 33
broch 121
broch of Gurness 120, 137, colour plate 16
broch-ology 120
brochs 91, 120–2
Bronze Age 19, 30, 44, 65–7, 71, 76, 91, 93, 95, 102, 107, 115, 120
Bronze Age ringwork 83
Bronze Age settlement 65, 80, 89, 96, 107, 109, 115, 120, 126
Broom Hill 42
brushwood platform 40
buckthorn 42
burial cairns 32
burials 65
Burren 71
Bury Hill 114
Butser Hill 94, 107, 135, colour plate 11

Caer Caradoc 100
Caerau hillfort 137
Caesar 93
calibration 47
calibration curve **9**, 27
Camborne 55
Camden 19
carbonised deposits 42
Carn Brea 51, 54–5, 94, 136
Carn Euny **77**, 110, 114, 136
Carn Goch 137

Carrock Fell 96, 135
Castle an Dinas 136
Castle Crag 135
catchment areas 41
cattle 119
cattle herding 67
causewayed enclosures 14
causewayed camp 43, 49, 51, 53, colour plate 1
Celts 91
cereal plants 43
cereal 63
Chalbury 103
chalk phallus 76
chambered tombs 14
Chilterns 53
Chysauster 136, colour plate 15, front cover
Claydon Pike 128
Cleveland 96
climate 17
cock fighting 125
cockles 35
Colchester 126
Collfryn **86**, **87**, 118
colonisation 37
concentric antenna enclosures 118
consumer site 40
contour fort 96
copper 65
Cornwall 45, 53–4
cow 59
crab-apple 63
crannogs 22, 91, 120–2
Crawford O.G.S. 20
cremated human bone 56
Crickley Hill 55, 94, 107, 136
crop marks **5**, **6**, 20, 22–3, 80, 91, 128
Crosby Ravensworth 135
CUCAP 22
Cueva de los Caballos 40
Culver Well 35
Cumbria **4**, 17, 33, 48–9, 60, 135

daggers 65
Danebury 22, **80**, **81**, 91, 93, 100, 109–10, 114, 136

Danube 65
Dartmeet **40**, 71
Dartmoor 15, 19, **40**, 65, 71, 75–6, 132
dating 22
Dean Moor 76
deer 42
defended hillforts 126
defended farmstead 119
dendrochronology **10**, 13, 27, 46
Denmark 49
deposition 63
Devon 53, 55
diffusion 65
documentary research 17
dogs 40
dolmens 14
domestic 14
domestic rubbish 54
domesticated grape 54
Doon Hill 62
Dorset 53, 55, 101
dresser 59
Dun Carloway 137
Dun Telve 120, 137
dung beetles 30
duns 91, 120, 122
Durham 96
Durotriges 104

earthworks 91
East Anglia 53
Ehenside Tarn **24**, 47
Eilean Domhnuaill 63
Eilean an Tighe 63
einkorn 54
elk 33
elm 41, 48–9
elm decline 30, 49
elm disease 49
elm leaves 49
emmer 54
enclosures 49, 91
England 11, 122, 132
environmental information 15, 17
Eston Nab 135
Etton **30**, 55
Europe 11
excavation 22

farmers 17, 132
farming 43, 45
Farmoor 129
farmsteads 91, 114
fauna 17
faunal assemblage 39
femur 40
Fengate 60, 71
Fens of East Anglia 15, **70**
field survey 22
field systems 91
fieldwork 93
Finavon 137
fire 33
fish 33, 35, 37, 59, 124
fish bait 59
Flag Fen 17, 90, 107, 136, colour plate 7

flint 40
flint knapping 35
flintworking 37
flora 17
flotation 29
foragers 43
foraging 41
forest clearance **18**, 41
France 15, 120
Fylde 38

geochemistry 22
geophysical survey **8**, 25
Gill Mill 128
glaciers 33
Glastonbury 91, **91**, 107, 122–3, colour
    plate 14
Glen Beag 121
glume wheats 119
goat 119–20
Goltho 71
Goring Gap 81
grains 63
Grassington 71
Great Urswick 135
Greenwell 19
Grimspound 136
Grimston-Lyles Hill 53
Grooved ware 60

Hallidale 121
Hambledon Hill **29**, 53–4, 94, 104, 136
hazel 42, 46, 63
hearths 37
Hebrides 63
Hembury 55
henge 43, 51
Highland Zone **2**, 15
hillforts **66**, **67**, 91, 94, 96
Hod Hill **68**, **72**, 100, 103, 136
Holland 120
Homo sapiens sapiens 32–3
horse 33
human adaptation 132
Humber 51
hunter-gatherer 33, 35, 43, 45, 132
hunting camp 39
hunting site 35

Industrial Revolution 127
Ingleborough hillfort **75**, 108, 135,
    back cover
Ingram valley 135
interpretation 132
interrupted ditch system **27**, 51
Ireland 11, 33, 71
Iron Age 14, 27, 30, 55, **61**, 76, 81, 86,
    91, 93, 101–3, 109, 121, 127, 130
Iron Age communities 91
Iron Age hillforts 94, 101, 110, 126
Iron Age round house 107, colour plate
    11
Iron Age settlement 91, 96, 124
Iron Age tribes **61**
Isle of Arran 61
Isle of Axholme 38

Isle of Man 96
Itford Hill **45**, 76–7

Jarlshof 137
jet bead 60

Kennet 63, 80–1
kill site 39–40
Kinder Scout 41
Kirkhead Cave 33
Knook Camp **1**

Ladle Hill **78**, **79**, 109
Lake Dwellings 22
Lake District 33, 122
land bridge **13**, 30, 37
landscape 15, 67
Langdale axe factory 47, 60–1
Lea Green, Grassington 85
Leskernick **39**, 71
Levi-Strauss 107
Lidbuy camp 100
lime 41
limpets 35, 59
Lindow Man 17
linear boundaries 65
linear reaves 72
lion 33
Loch Awe 121
lochs 22
long barrows 14, 43
Longridge Deverill Cow Down 93, 107,
    109
Lowland Zone **2**, 15
Lubbock 13

magnetometer 22
Maiden Castle **7**, 55, **65**, 91, 93–6, 100,
    102–3, 137
Mam Tor 135
mammoth 33
manuring 129
Marshall's Hill 80–1
Meare Heath bow **23**, 47
Meare Lake village 124
meat shortage 37
Mesolithic 30, 32, 35, 37, 39, 40–2, 48,
    81, 91, 127
Mesolithic settlement **15**, 35
metalworking 125
midden debris 55
middens 37, 132
Middle Bronze Age 77
Middle Ages 128
Mildenhall 56
Milfield basin 101
milk production 54
Mingies Ditches **95**, 128
mobile 43
modelling 132
Moel-y-Gaer 107
Montelius 32
monument 51
Mortimer 19
Morton 37
Mousa broch 138

Mucking **50**, 81, 94
Munro 22
mussels 37

National Records 19
Near East 43, 45
Neolithic 30, 35, 42–3, 45, 47–50, 53,
    55–6, 59, 115, 132
Neolithic Revolution 45
Norbury 99
Norfolk 71
North Uist 63
North York Moors 37, 39
North Sea 40
Northern Ireland 20
Northumberland 85, 96
Norton Fitzwarren 94
Norway 65
nuts 35

oak 28, 41–2, 48
oats 119
oblique photographs 22
oppida 101, 126
Ordnance Survey 20, 48, 67, 121
organic remains 37
Orkney 45, 57, 131
Oronsay **16**, 35
orthostat 55
ox 120
oysters 35

Paddock Hill, Thwing **51**, **52**, 82, 94
paddocks 128
palaeoenvironmental 30
Palaeolithic 11, 33, 35, 127
palimpsest 17
palynology 29
pannage 63
passage grave 14, 51
pastoralism 44
pattern of settlement 40
peas 124
peat bog 30
pig 37, 63, 119, 124
Piggot 20
Pike O'Stickle colour plate 4
Pimperne **64**, **83**, **84**, 93–4, 116
pine 41
pine marten 37
Plasketlands **8**, **25**, 48–9
pollen analysis 29
pollen diagram **11**, 29
poplar 42
Port Meadow 128
post-depositional factors 15
post-processual 44
pottery 31, 119, 125
Poundbury 103
pre-Saxon 15
prehistorians 14–5
prehistoric communities 33, 45
prehistoric landscapes 17, 90
prehistoric settlements 11, 13, 15, 17–9,
    21–2, 31–3, 44, 49, 67, 87, 94, 122,
    127, 131–3

Prehistoric Society 14, 140
probability theory 28
processual 44
promontory fort 96

Quarley Hill **82**, 115

radiocarbon dating **9**, 13, 27–8
RAF 22
Rams Hill 94
RCAHMS 140
RCAHMW 140
RCHME 20, 22, 76, 82, 114, 127, 132,
    140
red deer 33, 35, 37, 39, 59
reindeer 33
relative dating methods 22
Republic of Ireland 20
resistivity 22
Rhine 120
Rider's Ring **42**, 137
Ripon Tor **41**, 72
ritual 14
river gravels 79
roe deer 33, 37, 120
Romans 14, 19, 57, 93, 96, 126
Roman camp 53
Roman road 90, **93**, 124
Romano-British 15, 81
Rough Tor colour plate 5
round barrows 14, 19
round houses 91
Rox Hill 88
rubbish 37, 132

saddle quern 75
St Albans 126
Salisbury Plain **1**, 14
salmon 35
saunas 131
Saxon 81
Scotland 11, 15, 32–3, 96, 132
Scratchbury 101
sea trout 35
seabirds 37
seasonal sites 38
semi-mobile groups 43
settlements 65, 76
Severn valley 118
Shaugh Moor **43**, 75–6
sheep 59, 119
shell midden 35, 37
Silbury Hill 63
site formation processes 15
site catchment analysis 35
Skara Brae **31**, 57, 59, 64, 137
skeletons 54
Skomer Island **97**, 127, 131
small-scale excavation 22
SMR 20, 42
soil samples 30
Solway Plain 20, 48
Somerset Levels 15, 17, 30, 45, 48, 124
South Yorkshire 125
spatial analysis 13
spelt 124

spinning 125
Springfield Lyons 94
Staffordshire 51
Standrop Rigg **54**, 85–6
Stanton Harcourt **96**, 129
Staple Howe **88**, 120
Star Carr **17**, 38–40
Stepleton enclosure 54
stone box beds 59
stone built 59
stone circles 43
stone tools 37
Stone Age 33
Stonehenge **58**, **60**, 87–90, 101
Stones of Stenness 59
Stowe's Pound 136, colour plate 6
Stukeley 20
sturgeon 37
Suffolk 71
summer hunting sites 39
supermarket 33, 35
Sutton Common **92**, 125
Swaledale 71, 85
Swarthy Hill **4**
sweat boxes 131
Sweet Track **22**, 45–7, 49
Switzerland 22

technological change 65
Teesdale 40
Territorial analysis 35
territories 40
Thames valley 53, 80–1, 126–8, 131–2
theoretical models 17
thermoluminescent date 28
Thiessen polygons 13, **69**
Thorpe Thewles, 114 colour plate 12
Three Age system 11, 32
Tievebulliagh 61
Tiree 121
trade 94
transpiration 41
Tre'r Ceiri **73**, 105, 137
tree pollen 49
Trent 38
Trethellan Farm **44**, 76
Trundle 55, 137

Udal 63
uranium/thorium 28

Vale of Pickering 38
vegetational zones 30
Vespasian 100, 104
Victoria Cave 33

Wales 33, 116, 122, 127
Wardy Hill 101, colour plate 9
waterlogged 41, 55
Watkins Farm **95**, 128
wattles 42
Welland valley 55
Wessex 15, 53, 65
wheat 63, 120
whelks 37
whetstone 75

wild cat 37
wild fruit 35
wild ox 33
wild pig 33
willow 42
Windmill Hill **26**, 51, 53, 63, 94, 137
Winnal Down 109, 115
winter base camp 39

Woden Law **55**, 86, 138
Wolsty colour plate 2
wood working 42
Woodbury **62**, **63**, 93, 114
woodland clearance **18**, 41
Woolbury 114
woolly rhinoceros 33
wristguards 65

Yar Tor 72
Yeavering Bell **74**, 106, 136
Yorkshire Wolds 82, 85, 88
Yorkshire Dales 22, 107, 136

Zone of Survival 15
Zone of Destruction 15